W9-AOM-436

GOD IS RELEVANT

GOD IS RELEVANT

Finding Strength and Peace in Today's World

LUIS PALAU
and David Sanford

Doubleday

New York London Toronto Sydney Auckland

PUBLISHED BY DOUBLEDAY
a division of Bantam Doubleday Dell Publishing Group, Inc.
1540 Broadway, New York, New York 10036

DOUBLEDAY and the portrayal of an anchor with a dolphin are trademarks of Doubleday, a division of Bantam Doubleday Dell Publishing Group, Inc.

Book design by Chris Welch

Library of Congress Cataloging-in-Publication Data

Palau, Luis, 1934–
God is relevant : finding strength and peace in today's world / by Luis Palau and David Sanford. — 1st ed.
1. Apologetics. 2. Atheism—Controversial literature.
I. Sanford, David (David R.) II. Title.
BT1102.P234 1997
239′.7—dc21 97-1784
CIP

ISBN 0-385-48678-2

Printed in the United States of America
July 1997
First Edition
10 9 8 7 6 5 4 3 2 1

"To be always relevant, you have to say things which are eternal."
—Simone Weil

"He who marries the spirit of the age soon becomes a widower."
—Dean Inge

"All that is not eternal is eternally out of date."
—C. S. Lewis

"What we believe about God is the most important thing about us."
—A. W. Tozer

"You can say one thing for ignorance: it certainly causes a lot of interesting arguments."
—Anonymous (America)

"Non-thinking is an act of annihilation, a wish to negate existence, an attempt to wipe out reality."
—Ayn Rand

"Today's unthinkable becomes tomorrow's thinkable with remarkable speed."
—Francis Schaeffer

"A lie will travel around the world while truth is still putting on its boots."
—D. L. Moody

"Everybody's got a hungry heart."
—*Bruce Springsteen*

"To believe in heaven is not to run away from life; it is to run toward it."
—*Joseph D. Blinco*

"Psychology can teach us to be normal, but we must look elsewhere for the help we need to become human."
—*Harold Kushner*

"Trying to understand God is like trying to teach calculus to a worm."
—*Steven Myers*

"Life is a story without meaning told by an idiot."
—*Eugene Ionesco*

"God is dead. Marx is dead. And I don't feel so good myself."
—*Anonymous (France)*

"To believe in God is impossible, not to believe in Him is absurd."
—*Voltaire*

"If this is God's world, there are no unimportant people."
—*George Thomas*

CONTENTS

PREFACE

Big doors turn on small hinges.

The course of your life could change today based on a single decision you'll make, either consciously to lock God out of your life or to open the door of your heart and invite him to come in.

Right before the start of World War I, a French boy of seven or eight named Jean-Paul Sartre and his widowed mother were living with her parents. The grandfather was a Protestant, the grandmother a lifelong French Catholic (like my own maternal grandparents). At the dinner table, the family patriarch and matriarch often poked fun at each other's religious beliefs.

"No malice was involved," Jean-Paul later remembered. "Yet I concluded from these exchanges that the two faiths were equally valueless. Even though my family saw it as their duty to bring me up as a Catholic, religion never had any weight with me."

By the time the war ended, Jean-Paul had grown completely disenchanted with the Church. By the time he turned twelve, he thoroughly hated to attend mass and resolved that he would go no more.

To seal his decision that morning, Jean-Paul stood before a mirror and cursed God. Three times he damned his Creator and then felt a sense of relief. He was through with God and the Church. He decided to become an atheist so that he could live the rest of his days as he pleased.

Over the years, Sartre looked back at that event as a defining moment in his life. In *Being and Nothingness,* writing against certain Christian beliefs, he commented almost as an aside: "We should know for always whether a particular youthful experience had been fruitful or ill-starred, whether a particular crisis of puberty was a caprice or a real pre-formation of my later engagements; the curve of our life would be fixed forever."

In other words: if I really meant it when I cursed God, I thereby set the course of my entire life and sealed my fate.

Sartre went on to make a name for himself, of course. His political exploits are legendary, his writings definitive of mid-twentieth-century atheistic existentialism. Yet, reviewing his life, Sartre seems to swing between the extremes of heady pride and sexual liberation, on the one hand, and philosophical anguish and personal despair on the other.

On numerous occasions, Sartre stated that there is "no exit" from the human dilemma of trying to live as if God did not exist. "Man is alone," Sartre claimed, abandoned to his own destiny. "Hell is other people." Life is hard, and then you die. Period.

Shortly before Sartre's death, however, he relented. The *Nouvel Observateur* recorded a telling conversation between the famous existentialist and a Marxist writer.

Sartre told the journalist: "I do not feel that I am the product of chance, a speck of dust in the universe, but someone who was expected, prepared, prefigured. In short, a being whom only a Creator could put here; and this idea of a creating hand refers to God."

Sartre's former companion, Simone de Beauvoir, and other colleagues united in their consternation over such a "heretical" idea. But Sartre didn't care. When you're blind and dying, what's the use of playing hide-and-seek with reality?

How tragic that Sartre allowed a decision in his youth to overshadow any consideration of God's relevance for nearly six decades. He spent most of his years embittered against others, struggling in vain for joy, meaning, peace, and strength.

Although he's considered one of the greatest twentieth-century philosophers, Sartre committed two of this century's most prevalent errors of thinking.

First, he confused his *feelings* with *reality.* This happens all the time. A man wakes up one morning, rolls over, sees his wife, and realizes he doesn't have any loving feelings for her. This lack of feelings of love shocks him so much he decides it must be the truth. So he acts accordingly, forgetting that love is more than a momentary feeling. In reality, to love is a decision we make over and over again.

Second, Sartre confused an *event* with *fate.* When he cursed God, he felt he had sealed his destiny. There was no looking back, no recognition that he could choose otherwise. Until the very end of his life, Sartre cursed his fate as if he couldn't change it.

I don't know your particular life story. Yet after talking individually with thousands of people all across America and around the world, I find that many people wish, in their heart of hearts, that they could believe that God is relevant after all.

Maybe you've consciously cursed God. Maybe you've only rejected the Church. Maybe you've simply lacked the confidence to say, "God, if you're real, please make yourself real to me."

Like Sartre's father, my father (a successful businessman) died when I was only a boy. And like Sartre, as a twelve-year-old youth I too came to a point of decision. For the most part, my European forefathers had little to do with the Church. They debated religion and gave little or no thought to entering into a personal relationship with God. Would I follow their footsteps or not? One night, after reading from the Bible and talking it over with an older friend, I decided to open the door of my heart to God through Jesus Christ, by faith. Looking back, I now can see how that one decision revolutionized the course of my life.

Over the years, attending British boarding schools, emigrating to the United States for graduate studies, and now speaking in Olympic stadiums, concert halls, coliseums, and arenas to people all around the world, I've become absolutely convinced that God is immensely relevant to every area of life.

"Don't you ever have doubts?" I was asked again on national television while finishing the writing of this book. No, I honestly don't anymore. I've proved the relevance of God in my own experience, witnessed his transforming power in the lives of others, and confirmed our need for God while poring over the history of this past century and of those thinkers who have most shaped its course.

Yet this is *your* book, not only mine. I've written it, yes, but not with the purpose of saying, "Here's what I believe—take it or leave it."

Instead, I've sought to explore the roots and implications of today's postmodern disbelief, as a way of showing why Sartre, among others, ended up deciding that we *do* need God after all.

If Sartre could have done it all over, he would have lived for God, not against him. Yet why wait until the end of life to address life's most important question?

Whatever your background and experience, I invite you to explore whether God is indeed relevant as you and I, and our friends and loved ones, embark on a new century full of possibilities.

—*Luis Palau*

INTRODUCTION
(TO AMERICAN EDITION)

Intellectually, is it credible to say God is relevant?

The chairman of the editorial board of the *Encyclopaedia Britannica,* Mortimer J. Adler, was compelled to explain why "God" merited the longest essay in *The Great Books of the Western World* series. His reply to a critical reviewer bears pondering: "It is because more consequences for life follow from that one issue than from any other."

In this book, we'll ponder some of the important philosophical and practical ramifications that follow from "that one issue." In particular, we'll explore several questions of great consequence.

To begin with, we'll consider the profound philosophical implications of the question *Is God relevant?* If *not,* what are our options? Because so much else in life hinges on this "one issue," the opening chapters of this book tackle it head on and the closing chapters (Part III) take a closer look at the disturbing historical roots of postmodern *un*belief. Some readers may actually wish to read Part III first.

As well, in this book we'll consider the practical but nagging question *How is God relevant?* If indeed God exists, does he matter? In what ways? How does God relate to our deepest desires, our most profound needs, our greatest worries? Can I know him for myself? Can I have a personal, experiential *relationship* with the Creator of the universe?

This book may most intrigue not yet believing readers honest enough to inquire about what Will Durant calls the "greatest question of our time"—whether we can live without God. I realize, however, that some already believing readers may find certain sections of this book threatening to their faith.

For too long, some members of the Church have been afraid to face the causes of postmodern unbelief. But face it we must; otherwise any theology (system of belief in God) we claim evaporates into a cold mist, leaving us utterly naked, shivering, and alone, without hope in this world.

Admittedly, many people today *want* to go it alone, without God. They either feel no need for God, or they don't want God in their lives. Perhaps they've had a bad experience with organized religion. Or perhaps they have unanswered questions raised by some of modern history's most influential skeptics.

Rabbi Harold Kushner is right: "The past few centuries have not been kind to the cause of organized religion." But then again, is *religion* ultimately what matters?

What's ahead?

MASSIVE SPIRITUAL AWAKENING

In 1992, political theorist Francis Fukuyama gave us *The End of History.* Four years later, scientific analyst John Horgan brought us *The End of Science.* By the year 2000, will someone come out with *The End of Religion?*

Probably not.

As we near the turn of the millennium, religious fervor and spiritual interest are growing.

Religion is everywhere. National Public Radio, PBS, network television and cable networks, national news magazines such as *Time, Newsweek, U.S. News and World Report,* and major newspapers, including the *Wall Street Journal,* the *New York Times,* the *Los Angeles Times,* and *USA Today,* all continue to report on the interest in and growth of religion and spirituality in America.

To take the latest pulse of religion in America, the media often cite the findings of Princeton University's Center for the Study of American Religion, the Barna Research Group's reports, and other surveys. These research findings suggest the deeply ingrained bent of most Americans toward most things religious has become even more profound in recent years.

Around the globe, a greater percentage of the world's population believes in God now than at any other point in history. The conversion of hundreds of millions of individuals at the dawning of a new millennium is arguably one of the greatest sociological phenomena of this century.

The president of the Barna Research Group, George Barna, says, "Americans are probably more interested in spiritual matters than they have been in any other time in the past forty years."

In a lecture published in the *Wall Street Journal* and frequently quoted elsewhere, a leading economist, Robert Fogel of the University of Chicago, goes so far as to suggest we're already witnessing evidences of a "fourth great awakening" of religious fervor in America.

Of course, not all religious experiences are equal. Spirituality itself isn't always a good thing. If we all insist on doing our own thing, regardless of truth or consequences, I'm afraid the results could swing America's socioreligious pendulum in favor of agnosticism (skepticism about God) and atheism (unbelief in God).

If, however, the current interest in spirituality results in millions more people truly realizing that God is relevant, and entering into a personal relationship with him, the results could be profoundly positive. The history of previous religious awakenings in America and other nations bears this out.

WHAT DOES "GOD" MEAN?

In the late 1960s, one of the most popular campus buttons declared: "Leary is God." In the 1970s, George Burns played the role, cigar and all. More lately, Bill Gates has been up for top billing. During the 1996 NBA finals, *Time* magazine openly asked whether Michael Jordan is God.

When we say someone is "God," what do we mean? Unless we define our terms, you and I might think we understand each other yet be miles apart in our thinking.

"God talk" never has been easy. Ralph Waldo Emerson, for instance, had many great one-liners. One can't always be sure, however, what he meant. Take this classic line: "The simplest person, who in his integrity worships God, becomes God." Does Emerson mean that literally or figuratively? And what kind of God does he mean?

If I worship the biblical God who made heaven and earth and who is described in the Jewish and Christian Scriptures as holy and righteous and compassionate and true, for instance, do I become *like* God, exhibiting his attributes to some degree? Or does Emerson mean that, when I worship God, I'm simply worshiping myself? There's quite a difference!

A growing number of writers, leaders, and entertainers today publicly acknowledge that they worship "the god within." When they say "god," they are talking about themselves, in some sense. When I use the word "God" in this book, however, I'm thinking of God in the general sense of the Supreme Being and Creator of all things, or thinking of God in the particular sense of the God revealed in Jesus Christ and the biblical Scriptures. I'm not thinking of my ideal self, in any case.

RELIGIOUS SURFING ON THE NET

In the wake of the latest advances in the information revolution, religious writer Mart De Haan says humanity's newest temptation is to look into our computer screens and "imagine that with enough knowledge we will be able to solve all of our problems" and "act as if knowledge is God."

De Haan isn't implying that God isn't on the Net. He's there, all right—laughing, weeping, whispering in our ear, trying to get our attention.

Within two years of the Internet going public, users had created more than 56,000 sites that used God in their descriptions, 5,700 more made references to the Hindu gods Vishnu and Shiva, and another 4,500 referred to the Islamic god Allah.

A few months later, *Time* reported: "If you instruct AltaVista, a powerful Internet search engine, to scour the Web for references to Microsoft's Bill Gates, the program turns up an impressive 25,000 references. But ask it to look for Web pages that mention God, and you'll get 410,000 hits. Look for Christ on the Web, and you'll find him—some 146,000 times."

Of course, some of the attention God has been getting on the Net isn't complimentary. On the *God* Web page, a convert to atheism cynically refers to his childhood beliefs—fostered by family members and "a few respectable, intelligent" religious figures—and proclaims his liberation from those beliefs, thanks to "reason."

On the *Atheistic Manifesto* Web site, Jeffrey Clark gives twenty-three reasons why he "operationally believes that there is no God," though, he says, he's "not 100% certain." His reasons include the "thousands of differing religious belief structures which are mutually exclusive and equally believable," scientific progress over the past four centuries, and his dislike of Church teachings.

On the *God Within* page, Chris Moran tries to explain to his mother—and other believers—why he chooses to become a free, intelligent, substance-free, and happy person "without the fiction forced on feeble minds." Although an atheist, "I sure as heck believe in a greater power within myself. I propagate that power with every feat I accomplish that amazes me. *I* do it, not some deity or outer power."

On the *How's Your Jesus Christ Been Hanging?* site, someone has compiled an assortment of disturbing quotes for atheism and against the Christian God, including this zinger from Jules Renard: "I don't know if God exists, but it would be better for His reputation if He didn't."

So how is God's reputation doing these days, anyway?

PLURALISTIC AMERICA

If we believe the pollsters, the United States is largely a "Christian" nation. A phenomenal four out of five American adults claim to be Christians.

That self-described (though undefined) faith seems to be widely represented at all demographic levels. George Gallup, Jr., notes: "The United States is unique in that it has one of the highest levels of formal education in the world, and at the same time, one of the highest levels of religious faith."

Not surprisingly, most Americans have a high view of the Christian faith. According to the Barna Research Group, eighty-five percent of American adults think Christianity has a positive impact on society. Even among non-Christians, seventy-seven percent have a favorable opinion of Christianity.

Sadly, other religious faiths were not as highly regarded: the percentage of respondents to the Barna survey who had a positive view of Jews, only fifty-eight percent; of Buddhists, forty-five percent; of Mormons, forty-three percent; of Muslims, forty percent; and of atheists, thirteen percent.

I'm no advocate of what Drew University ethics professor Thomas C. Oden has called "compulsive hypertolerationism." Yet such statistics (and the massive number of religious martyrs worldwide, in the tens of thousands each year) show a deplorable lack of religious toleration today.

Atheists, of course, get the worst rap. They always have. Plato suggested atheists comprise such a grave danger to society that, if convicted twice of "impiety," they should be executed.

Philosopher John Locke argued against granting equal civil rights to unbelievers since—lacking any fear of God or future judgment—they seldom abide by "promises, covenants, and oaths, which are the bonds of human society."

In both Britain and the United States, Locke's argument was used for years to prevent such individuals from taking public office or testifying in court.

CIVIL SPEECH

The president and CEO of the Corporation for Public Broadcasting, Ervin Duggan, notes that often today discourse is "angry and inconclusive." In writing this book I have tried to heed his call for civil speech.

Still, I recognize that some may object to my use of certain words and phrases. Interestingly, I find that many who argue the loudest against the validity of even asking questions of truth often see no contradiction in setting themselves up as judges of the worthiness of half the English language. Have we forgotten the warning of Orwell's *1984* already?

Some so-called theologians (religious experts), who should know better, traffic in Newspeak with the best of them. An editorial in the *Wall Street Journal* put it well: "It's pretty pathetic to watch theologians waste their time worrying that a left-handed, blind, black woman might somehow think the Bible excludes her, when the main message of the text teaches exactly the opposite. Apparently the contemporary equivalent of pondering how many angels can fit on the head of a pin is to calculate the number of [politically incorrect] words in the Bible."

I have no interest in either confusing issues of truth or putting my own spin on certain words. And I certainly don't expect you to agree with everyone I quote and everything I say in this book. I simply ask that we agree to interpret what's said on these pages according to Webster's or any other standard English-language dictionary.

In this book, you'll read compelling statements against and for the relevance of God. You'll have an opportunity to consider the direct claims of many leading skeptics (Part III) and decide for yourself whether to trust God and enter into relationship with him.

William James once said, "A great many people think they are thinking when they are really rearranging their prejudices." This book aims to help readers think by first exploring what our postmodern prejudices *might be,* then examining whether those prejudices *make sense.*

INTENDED READERS

During the course of hundreds of press conferences and interviews, reporters have asked me repeatedly to discuss whether God is relevant in today's postmodern culture. I'm always happy to do so, for I find the topic somewhat complicated but thoroughly intriguing. Why? Because I believe the evidence is overwhelming that God exists, that he is relevant, and that he longs for relationship with you and me.

If this book should be read anywhere, it is in the libraries of the world's great universities, where belief in God has been ridiculed by certain learned professors. It should be read in the bookshops of the world's great cities, where the consequences of unbelief are most evident in today's older populations and youth. It should be read in the headquarters of the "mainline" denominations sidelined in recent years in part by stark disbelief in once cherished orthodox creeds.

It should be read in homes by thoughtful men and women serious about rediscovering the Christian faith that their parents (or grandparents) chose to relinquish for certain personal reasons. It should be read by those who have gone through a divorce that seems irrational, who wonder what went wrong and if God could make it right again somehow. It should be read by individuals struggling with alcoholism, drugs, sexual addictions, or other destructive habits who wonder, "Is God there? Can I find him? Will he change me?"

It should be read by students of history, politics, psychology, and religion who know the twentieth century went wrong, who feel upset at the epidemic social problems we're facing today, and who fear the next century will be only worse.

It should be read over the Net by atheists and theists, by agnostics and believers who wish to interact with the themes of the book and cast their votes at http://www.gospelcom.net/lpea.

As you read this book, I hope you'll find to your profound satisfaction that God is relevant. If you do, please write and tell me. Even if you don't, let me know your specific questions or concerns (see page 120).

SYNCRETISTIC APPROACH

You may be an agnostic or atheist, a Buddhist or Catholic, a Hindu or Jew, Protestant or Shintoist, or something else. In the course of reading this book, you may lose your religion or decide to pursue an ongoing relationship with God. The choice is yours.

The fact is, you may currently embrace a host of diverse beliefs.

New York Times religion writer Gustav Niebuhr says today we're witnessing "a mass movement of individual seekers." More and more, people are shunning labels, exercising the personal right to draw good from several seemingly contradictory belief systems. As if sincerity is the greatest virtue—as if it's impossible to be sincerely *wrong.*

Syncretism (combining parts of different belief systems) is very much in vogue, frustrating the most careful efforts of the U.S. Census Bureau, United Nations, and others who seek to divide humanity mathematically into precisely labeled groups.

Pick-and-choose religion is all the rage, even if it doesn't always make sense. R. C. Sproul writes: "Most of us are inconsistent about such matters. Our viewpoint comes from the melting pot. We get mixed up. Our pot has a dash of faith and a dash of skepticism. We are at once religious and secular. We believe in God, sometimes. Our religion has elements of superstition at some times and is tempered by sober science at other times."

Such an approach is confusing at best. Sproul continues: "On Sunday we say the creed. On Monday we are fatalists. We try to separate our religious life from the rest of our life. We live by holding contradictory beliefs. Living in contradictions can be exciting. Life is surely more than logic. But the contradictory life is a confusing life, a life of inconsistency and incoherence. Its bottom line is chaos.

"We are inconsistent and confused because we fail to understand where Christianity ends and paganism begins. We do not know where the boundary lines are."

One place where those boundary lines have been clear, however, is in the Academy.

SECULARIZED ACADEMY

Is it wrong that our institutions of higher learning seek to secularize (take religious belief away from) today's brightest and best? Marty Kaplan, a former speechwriter for Vice-President Walter Mondale and now a Hollywood screenwriter and producer, says no: "If Harvard had made me a more spiritual person, it would have failed in its promise to socialize me to the values of the educated élite. Those values are secular."

Kaplan goes on to say: "The prized act of mind in the Academy is the laying bare of hidden agendas. The educated person knows that love is really about libido, that power is really about class, that judgment is really about politics, that religion is really about fantasy, that necessity is really about chance. These views come from an Enlightenment that began with Galileo and Newton and a modernity begun by Darwin, Marx and Freud. We are Nietzsche's children, shivering in the pointless void."

A self-described "cultural Jew, an agnostic, a closet nihilist," Kaplan ventured forth from Harvard to face the life of a postmodernist: "Of course I didn't like it. Who wants to face death without God? Who wants to tell the kids that the universe is indifferent to them? But the alternative—faith—was unavailable to me. Once the mind thinks some thoughts, it cannot unthink them."

Kaplan's last statement is bold, quotable, and thankfully untrue. Our minds are not CD-ROMs. We can rewrite old scripts, unlearn half truths, embrace new revelations, reach new heights that surpass old understandings.

Nevertheless, Kaplan has a point: the writings of Charles Darwin, Karl Marx, Friedrich Nietzsche, Sigmund Freud, and others have had a profound effect on our culture. Many postmodernists, including Kaplan, have sought to fill the aching void in their hearts, only to be "ambushed by spirituality."

Consider what Steven Muller, former president of Johns Hopkins University, says: "The failure to rally around a set of values means that universities are turning out potentially highly skilled barbarians." Pharmacokinetics researchers without scruples. Wall Street MBAs without souls.

Theologian John H. Gerstner takes Muller's point a step further: "Suppose, for example, that the generality of men believed that the exact sciences were merely games (Abel), that nothing was worthwhile except art, sex, and a few other tangible pleasures (Dreiser), and that the beginning and end of thought was complete and unyielding despair (Bertrand Russell)." Of what value, then, is higher education?

Educator Bruce Wilkinson reminds us that the founders of Harvard, Princeton, Yale, Dartmouth, Brown, and other influential Ivy League schools had the stated objective of furthering the Christian faith for the good of America. In the original articles of incorporation and bylaws, they declared that God has no grandchildren: each new generation must embrace faith in God for itself.

But what happened? Each university actively sought to Christianize America after its founding. But eventually they let go of conversion Christianity, in deference to others, so as not to offend those of other persuasions. What began with earnest Christian *conviction* within a generation became mere *tradition.* Later, *skepticism* (doubt of basic religious principles) and then *unbelief* overtook each of America's most prestigious educational institutions. Unbelieving professors eventually made routine mockery of once cherished beliefs.

The same pattern emerges throughout the history of most (not all) of America's other great Christian institutions. Today, for instance, many have no idea that the YMCA began as the Young Men's Christian Association, one of the nineteenth century's premiere evangelical organizations. Few recall the International Red Cross's distinct Christian heritage. Few remember the religious foundations of the vast majority of America's leading hospitals.

TIME TO RESCUE GOD?

Thomas Luckmann, a sociologist of religion, says: "There is scarcely anything which has been declared dead as often as religion." When people recognize that life without God is hell, spirituality always makes a comeback.

In recent times, that comeback has been evident on the *New York Times Book Review* best-seller lists. Those lists have consistently included eight to twelve or more titles with religious themes, including a New Age novel, *The Celestine Prophecy* by James Redfield, and an inspirational paperback, *The Road Less Traveled* by M. Scott Peck, on the list a phenomenal five hundred thirty-one weeks longer than any other book.

No stranger to the best-seller list is Kushner, author of *Who Needs God* and rabbi of Temple Israel in Natick, Massachusetts. Kushner says that, "for the religious mind and soul, the issue has never been the existence of God but the importance of God, the difference that God makes in the way we live. . . . A God who exists but does not matter, who does not make a difference in the way you live, might as well not exist. . . . The issue is not what God is like. The issue is what kind of people we become when we attach ourselves to God."

The current cultural trend toward spirituality affirms a truth echoed down through the centuries: that we are somehow incomplete, somehow unfulfilled, without God.

H. G. Wells once observed: "The religion of the atheist has a God-shaped blank at its heart."

Before committing suicide, Ernest Hemingway admitted: "I live in a vacuum as lonely as a radio tube when it is dead, and there is no plug to get life from."

On one of her visits, Mother Theresa said, "There is a famine in America." Not a famine of food, but of love, of truth, of life.

Philip Berman echoes these sentiments in his probing *Chicago Tribune* magazine essay "Search for Meaning." Berman writes: "ours is neither a financial, social or political problem, but rather a spiritual problem. There is a desperate hunger for meaning in the late 20th Century that shiny new cars apparently can't satisfy."

To back up his point, Berman quotes Ivy League professor Cornel West, who says that a "pervasive spiritual impoverishment grows" in America. He also cites former National Security Adviser Zbigniew Brzezinski's observation that our nation is gripped by a virulent spiritual malaise fueled "largely by cornucopian aspirations devoid of deeper human value."

Former Secretary of the U.S. Department of Education William Bennett agrees: "During the last three decades, American society has experienced substantial social regression . . . something has gone wrong at the core."

Billy Graham has made it clear: "It's either back to the Bible or back to the jungle." The jungle is creeping up on us.

Carl F. H. Henry, the first editor of *Christianity Today,* puts it this way: "The barbarians are coming." Without a massive turning to God, Henry foresees "barbarians" taking over our land. Not foreigners, but our own unrepentant generation, plus our children and grandchildren, living without God Almighty as the ruler of their lives.

The problem is in the heart, not simply the outward behavior that so alarms us during every news report. God says, "The heart is deceitful above all things, and desperately wicked." (You'll find this verse in the Bible, book of Jeremiah, chapter 17, verse 9.)

I believe what's needed is not more good advice dished out in the newspaper and on television, but the good news that "Christ died for our sins" (1 Corinthians 15:3).

In this book, I show that God is immensely relevant because he (and he alone) can forgive our sins, fill the void within our souls, give us peace and strength, and offer us the assurance of eternal life and heaven. What's your experience? Are you ready to consider God's relevance in your own life? I'm so glad you've picked up this book. I invite you now to turn to Chapter One and read with an open heart. Keep a pen on hand to record your thoughts, and write to me when you're finished. I look forward to hearing from you.

GOD IS RELEVANT

Part I

THE PRESENT SITUATION

CHAPTER 1

GOD MAKES A COMEBACK

God is relevant—even if you don't want him to be.

I saw this firsthand in London, where I had the privilege of speaking with members of the British royal family and to 528,000 others about the question "Is God Relevant?"

The question became all the rage in the British press during that speaking tour, with the newly appointed Anglican Bishop of Durham, the Rev. David Jenkins, openly casting doubt on some of classic Christianity's most important theological claims about the virgin birth, the resurrection of Jesus Christ—anything to do with the miraculous.

Not that the reverend bishop was the first contemporary religious leader to raise such questions. The Rev. John A. T. Robinson, Anglican Bishop of Woolwich, provoked a great deal of controversy with his 1963 book, *Honest to God.*

Not since Robinson, however, had an Anglican bishop captured such prominent media attention. Stories in the *Economist,* the *Wall Street Journal,* and other publications focused international attention on this controversy. Especially after the York Minster cathedral (the largest Gothic cathedral in Britain) was struck by a bolt of lightning less than three days after the Bishop of Durham's consecration there.

Was such an "act of God" divine retribution for the Rev. Jenkins's remarks? Many people, including the bishop himself, emphatically denied that God has any dealings with life on planet Earth.

Upon what grounds does the postmodernist determine whether "God talk" any longer makes sense? In part, it depends on what you mean by *God.* Does it mean anything at all? Around the world, through the ages, both belief and unbelief have marched side by side.

EXPERIMENTAL SPIRITUALITY

As we saw in the Introduction, Americans are more interested in matters of faith today than at any other time in the past four decades. While interest in spirituality is rising, however, it's often only experimental. Americans are dabbling in all things religious, often more concerned about their experiences (how they *feel*) than about facts (what is *true*).

As a result, many individuals today see no contradiction in creating their own pick-and-choose, syncretistic religion. I saw this again recently when one of my city's most brilliant business leaders was diagnosed with cancer. Before he died a week later, this well-beloved gentleman, Bill Naito, planned portions of his own memorial. He insisted on prayers from a Buddhist priest, a Catholic priest, a Jewish rabbi, and a Methodist minister. Naito's brother Sam told the more than one thousand attending the service that Bill "wasn't sure which God he would meet in heaven."

What about you? If you knew you had only one week to live, what would be your claim to faith? The bottom line is you can be any religion you want to be . . . if what you believe about God corresponds to reality. After all, God isn't Buddhist (traditional Buddhists don't even believe in God; they're atheists by definition). God isn't Catholic, Jewish, or Methodist either. The question ultimately isn't who *owns* God but who God *is*.

WISDOM TRADITIONS

In the PBS five-part series *The Wisdom of Faith,* host Bill Moyers featured Huston Smith, whom *Newsweek* calls "a genial, white-bearded pioneer in the study of world religions" and "the original New Age spiritual surfer."

Throughout the series, Smith tells personal stories of his experiences with the six "wisdom traditions"—Confucianism, Hinduism, Buddhism, Judaism, Christianity, and Islam.

One of Smith's best one-liners echoes throughout the series: "The enduring religions at their best contain the distilled wisdom of the human race." This is a popular but useless idea, some critics claim—sweet icing deliciously spread across an otherwise stale cupcake.

Writer Kenneth L. Woodward minces no words in discounting the validity of such syncretism: "Smith's own distilled wisdom seems to be that all spiritual truths point to the same transcendent truth. Only the packaging is different. That's a very democratic assumption. After all, there is no karma in Christianity, no Creator in Buddhism. In short, ideas do matter in religion."

True, the "wisdom traditions" Smith extols do not agree with each other. Still, syncretism abounds, even if it doesn't make sense rationally. According to David Fried of Cambridge, Massachusetts, in a letter to *Time,* "One thing common to all religions is the search for truth." It's the journey that's important, we're told, not any particular destination. In real life, that never works for long.

In his book *The Search for God,* David Manning White claims each of the great world religions originated from a common divine source. In his readings, White says, "I encountered the beauty and wisdom of the Koran, the hymns of Kabir and Guru Nanakk, the sacred poetry of Jalal-ud-din Rumi, the moral revelations of Gautama Buddha, and the countless jewels of the Vedic literature of India. Reading these gems of spirituality and comparing their approaches to understanding God with those in the Old and New Testaments convinced [him] that one supreme creator was the author who inspired all God Seekers."

In an effort to affirm those of various faiths, White ends up offending at least eighty percent of the world's population, who strongly disagree that God is the author of such confusion.

Some believe this individualistic approach to spirituality may create more new religions in America within the next fifteen years than in the entire past century, as "newly enlightened" persons start marketing whatever peculiar combination of religious ideas they have concocted. The situation here is not unlike India, where countless religions and more than three hundred million gods flourish.

As a consequence, Episcopal bishop William Swing has toured the world to drum up support for what he calls the United Religions, which he envisions as a united world church.

Religious diversity does indeed have its advocates. Yet what about the contradictions between different belief systems? Rabbi Harold Kushner says, "Religions can disagree and still each be true because people's spiritual needs come in different forms." Is that statement itself true?

In today's pick-and-choose environment, any appeal to religious authority apparently has been lost on at least half a generation. We're driven by impulse, not conviction. We treat spiritual choices like shopping at a mall. Today, let's eat at McDonald's. Tomorrow, at Burger King. As if religious choices have little or no consequence.

We're hungry, all right. Our search is real. Many are finding peace and strength by opening the doors of their hearts to God. Yet many others are naively open to *anything*.

The key is finding relationship with God himself, personally. We're reminded of this in the words of Moses, the prophet, who said that if "you seek the LORD your God, you will find him if you look for him with all your heart and with all your soul" (Deuteronomy 4:29).

In reaction to the glut of new cults and isms aggressively vying for our affections, a significant segment of the American population is retreating back to the supposed safety and sanity of some of the older, established religious institutions. Their search is important. Their intentions are sincere and well-meaning. Yet have the older, traditional religions filled the spiritual hunger of the masses? No, not always. Religious exercises can wear thin. This latest trend, like syncretism, may eventually lead to renewed spiritual frustration for some.

Has religion always been this confusing?

Unfortunately, yes.

ANCIENT GODS OF FANTASY

When it comes to gods and goddesses, the ancient Greeks had their hands full with numerous fantastic deities of mythic proportions.

Aeschylus (525–456 B.C.), often considered the classical founder of tragedy, wrote a forceful Greek myth titled *Prometheus Bound.* In this tragic play, Aeschylus tells the story of a brave Titan, Prometheus, who stole fire from the gods and gave it to humans. It seems Prometheus did the deed as much to spite the overlord Zeus as to benefit humanity.

As Aeschylus tells the story, Zeus punished the despised Titan by ordering him chained to a rock and then sending a great eagle to eat away at his liver. Despite such torment, Prometheus refused to yield to the will of Zeus and ultimately was rescued by Hercules, son of Zeus.

In the spirit of Prometheus, the classical Greek philosopher Protagoras (fifth century B.C.) openly admitted: "As to the gods, I am unable to say whether they exist or do not exist." He was the original agnostic—and for good reason. The ancient Greek gods were wild fantasies of the mind, imaginative folk tales that captured the hearts of a noble people. Yet such gods proved useless, meaningless, and irrelevant both to this life and to the call of eternity.

By nature, men and women yearn to worship *something.* The Greek myths about Zeus, Hera, Hercules, Hermes, and other gods tried to fill that void. Protagoras was honest enough to say such fantasies were ridiculous; they did nothing for him.

Like Protagoras and other educated Greeks, Socrates (470?–399 B.C.) also rejected the veneration of Zeus and his tribe. For this crime, he was condemned to death as *atheos,* as godless. Yet Socrates was no atheist—he had rejected belief in wild myths, not God per se. He actually spoke of the existence of one true God before his death.

From a handful of twelfth-century manuscripts, copied more than fourteen hundred years after his death, we're reminded that Aristotle (384–322 B.C.) found it impossible to believe that any god should be concerned with humanity. To him, God was an impersonal force, a first cause or prime mover, uninterested in human affairs.

From another handful of ninth-century manuscripts, however, we learn that Plato (427–347 B.C.) actively promoted a new set of religious ideals.

While Plato's abstract and vague ideals didn't immediately spark the religious imagination of his people, wisdom traditions were taking shape in other parts of the ancient world.

CONFUCIANISM: GOD?

What about Confucianism? Will it help us find God? Again, no.

In China, a philosopher named Confucius (sixth century B.C.) taught his people a profound code of cultural, spiritual, and moral ethics. In many ways, Confucius taught the value of revering tradition but did initiate several reforms.

One reform convinced the early Chinese emperors not to order the killing of wives, concubines, and associates upon their majesties' deaths. Such practices had been meant to ensure the well-being of the deceased emperors in the next life. Instead, Confucius advocated placing clay models of the living in the late emperors' tombs.

By what he doesn't say in his writings, however, Confucius reveals doubts about the afterlife, let alone the existence of any gods. Religious writer John Gerstner notes that, while Confucianism "pays nominal adherence to traditional Chinese polytheism and ancestor worship," it's "basically agnostic."

In any case, Confucius certainly didn't advocate the propagation of any new religions. He left that up to China's animist neighbors to the west, on the Indian subcontinent.

HINDUISM: MANY GODS

Will Hinduism lead us to know the living and true God? Hardly.

Unlike other wisdom traditions, Hinduism is a multiplicity of polytheistic religions (embracing many gods) and pantheistic philosophies (equating what is with God). These were lumped many, many centuries later (some say rather rudely) by British overlords into a single religious entity called "Hinduism," something many Hindus admit they couldn't define if you paid them.

Hinduism has no founder, let alone a common creed. You can believe almost anything and call yourself a good Hindu. Syncretism reigns supreme. This doesn't sit well with some in the West, but in India it very much makes sense.

Want to practice yoga at home and meditate on your personal mantra by the hour? Fine. Want to study sophisticated Sankhya philosophy at the local university this semester? Go ahead. Want to be a religious ascetic? Admirable. Want to indulge in ritual sex? It's your life. Want to bathe in the Ganges River modestly dressed in a ceremonial red robe? Do it. Want to dance through the marketplace wearing nothing? Fine.

Want to add Jesus to the list of gods you worship? That's fine too. Unless you take seriously Jesus Christ's claims that forgiveness of sins and eternal life are his alone to bestow—because of his crucifixion and resurrection—on those who believe in him and receive him by faith.

I remember flying on Air India, conversing with a distinguished Indian judge. He was very well traveled, with two daughters working as attorneys in the United States and Britain. As we conversed, I told him about my work speaking on the relevance of Jesus Christ all around the world. He looked at me and said, "The moment you sat down, I saw an aura around your head." Later in the conversation he told me, "If you lived in India, I'd follow you as my guru." Not that I want to be anyone's guru, believe me! But my point is this: anyone with charisma and some sort of following can start a new sect of Hinduism, if he or she wishes.

In some ways, India always has rivaled ancient Greece in its religious imagination. You feel an intense spirituality envelop you the moment you arrive. The ease with which you can start a conversation on spiritual issues among the Hindus is remarkable to anyone from America or Europe who knows and loves God.

I've found one cannot walk the streets of India's great cities, taking in the sights and smelling the incense-laden air, without immediately becoming fascinated by the nation's incredible religious diversity. Shrines of every shape and size—some mammoth—promote the worship of countless deities represented by colorful works of art.

Behind India's millions of deities, Hindus worship an ultimate divine essence or presence, Brahman. To disparage any particular deity, considered a manifestation of Brahman, is unacceptable. Tolerance of any and all religious claims is a sacred Hindu virtue.

The honorable Mahatma Gandhi, who did so much to free India politically, emphasized this Hindu ideal when he said: "I believe in the Bible as I believe in the Gita. I regard all the great faiths of the world as equally true with my own. It hurts me to see any one of them caricatured as they are today by their own followers." By "believe," I think I'm correct in assuming Gandhi meant that he respected both the Bible and the Gita. In any case, I'm confident he didn't hold that they teach the same theological ideas, for they contradict one another thoroughly about the very nature of God.

Likewise, India's former president Sarvepalli Radhakrishnan reinforced this concept by recounting the popular legend of the blind beggars examining an elephant: one feels a leg and "sees" a tree trunk, one feels the tail and "sees" a rope, one feels an ear and "sees" a palm leaf, and so on.

The point of the story, Radhakrishnan said: "In theological discussions we are at best blind beggars fighting with one another. The complete vision is difficult and the Buddhas are rare."

Yet if God has in fact revealed himself, as nearly half the world's population believes, then the analogy of the blind feeling for God is meaningless.

Jesus himself warned, "If a blind man leads a blind man, both will fall into a pit" (Matthew 15:14).

BUDDHISM: NO GODS

Buddhism has become popular among some in the West, but it also fails to lead us to know God our creator personally.

In northern India, a royal prince named Siddhartha Gautama (563?–?483 B.C.) sought the meaning of life. After becoming disenchanted with traditional polytheistic and pantheistic Hinduism, he spent several years in solitary contemplation. Upon achieving what he considered spiritual enlightenment at the age of thirty-five, while sitting under a bodhi tree, Gautama Buddha embarked on founding a new religion of self-denial and universal brotherhood, without any reference to God the Creator or any other so-called gods.

Buddhism, then, as a philosophy without God, began as a reform movement over and against Hinduism. As a foundation for this new religion, Gautama taught "the Four Noble Truths" and "the Noble Eightfold Path," which emphasize the achievement of spiritual liberation from the suffering caused by humanity's willfulness, selfishness, and lust by walking the "middle road."

In Hong Kong, Singapore, Taiwan, Thailand, and other Asian nations, I have seen how marvelously this middle road encourages Buddhist adherents to be gentle, courteous, and obsequious. Yet whenever I visit these nations to speak on God's relevance, people fill arenas by the thousands and stadiums by the tens of thousands. Why? Because something in Buddhism is missing: it offers no hope beyond tomorrow.

The classic goal of Buddhism is to escape this life, to become one with the universe, and thus to achieve nirvana—nothingness. Only then, Gautama said, will we be free from the pain life brings.

Not that Buddhism lacks spirituality. A prominent element in popular Buddhism is the fear of curses and of spirits bringing trouble on families, businesses, or other groups.

Like Jesus, Gautama never committed his teachings to writing. He left that to his followers. In essence, his is more a man-centered philosophy of life than a spiritual system of worship of the living God.

In recent centuries, one branch of Buddhism, the Mahayana, has considered Siddhartha Gautama a god. But as far as we can tell, the original Buddha never taught about god, nor saw himself as one. It's reported that shortly before his death, Gautama admitted he was still searching for the truth.

Only in the prophetic, monotheistic world religions do we discover that God is relevant.

JUDAISM: ONE GOD

What about Judaism?

In many ways, I deeply admire this oldest of the monotheistic world religions. I read its Scriptures faithfully. These very Scriptures describe the temptation we all face to worship something—anything—rather than the true God.

During the Buddha's lifetime, for instance, a handful of prophets warned the Israelite people of the dire consequences of not repenting of their sins against the Lord God. These prophets ministered among the people during the Jewish Babylonian exile (605–536 B.C.), and other prophets followed for more than a century, continually pointing the "wayward" back to the Lord God, YHWH, the one and only Creator of all things.

What sins did these prophets warn against? Basically, that from theism the Israelite people had turned to apathetic deism (God doesn't care about us/why should we care about him?), then to outright agnosticism (antisupernaturalism) or blatant paganism and idolatry (worshiping man-made "gods" in place of the one true God). This cycle of gradual apostasy and prophetic calls back to the worship of YHWH recurs throughout the Hebrew Scriptures:

"The idols of the nations are silver and gold, made by the hands of men. They have mouths, but cannot speak, eyes, but they cannot see; they have ears, but cannot hear, nor is there breath in their mouths. Those who make them will be like them, and so will all who trust in them" (Psalm 135:15–18).

"To whom then will you compare God? What image will you compare him to? As for an idol, a craftsman casts it, and a goldsmith overlays it with gold and fashions silver chains for it. A man too poor to present such an offering selects wood that will not rot. He looks for a skilled craftsman to set up an idol that will not topple" (Isaiah 40:18–20).

"All who make idols are nothing, and the things they treasure are worthless. Those who would speak up for them are blind; they are ignorant, to their own shame. Who shapes a god and casts an idol, which can profit him nothing? He and his kind will be put to shame; craftsmen are nothing but men. Let them all come together and take their stand; they will be brought down to terror and infamy" (Isaiah 44:9–11; see also 44:12–20).

This cycle of idolatry and prophetic calls for repentance continued after the completion of the canon of the inspired Hebrew Scriptures. In the second century before Christ, for instance, the Maccabeus clan again called the Israelites back to YHWH, the Lord, leading a rebel force that regained control of the desecrated Jewish temple from the Greek infidel Antiochus Epiphanes, on December 25, 165 B.C.

After centuries of oppression, in A.D. 70 the nation of Israel was dismantled when the Roman Empire destroyed its cities and dispersed the surviving remnant of its people among the nations. Unlike any other dispersed ancient people, however, the Jewish race maintained its own identity vigilantly until modern Israelis could establish a new homeland nearly nineteen centuries later, in 1948. All this had been prophesied clearly and has, amazingly, come about in our generation before our very eyes.

The founding of the Jewish faith itself dates back long before Buddha and Confucius, more than four thousand years, to Abraham (twentieth century B.C.). Called the father of the world's three great monotheistic religions, Abraham was born into a polytheistic southern Mesopotamian family, approximately 220 miles southeast of Baghdad.

According to the Hebrew Bible, YHWH revealed himself to Abraham, calling him to leave the city of Ur and "go to the land I will show you" (Genesis 12:1). Thus begins one of the most famous narratives in what is perhaps the oldest of the monotheistic Scriptures.

True to life, the Hebrew Scriptures don't paint Abraham as an instant stellar model of faith. At various turns he doubts the Lord God, tries to save his own skin, and struggles in other ways for almost four decades before finally demonstrating a profound and settled faith in the Lord God.

The same Scriptures paint a very human portrait of the great Israelite deliverer, Moses (fourteenth century B.C.). The Jewish psychoanalyst Sigmund Freud thoroughly embraced atheism, yet found this great religious leader fascinating. Freud spent part of the last five years of his life writing a book about this man, whom he considered the true "founder" of Judaism.

The storytelling power of the Hebrew Bible—known among Christians as the Old Testament—is probably unmatched in all of literature. Even the fanatical atheist Friedrich Nietzsche, of "God is dead!" fame, read it with deep admiration.

Today, of course, Judaism encompasses a variety of religious movements—Orthodox, Conservative, Reconstructionist, and Reform. Many Christians find it surprising that these four theologically diverse groups, as well as a healthy number of agnostics and atheists, sometimes may all be members in good standing at a local synagogue.

Almost against all hope, traditional Orthodox Jewish believers still await the long-prophesied Messiah, God's Anointed One, their promised Redeemer. Two thousand years ago, that hope gave birth to what is now the world's largest religious faith.

EARLY CHRISTIANITY: GOD WITH US

Can we come to know God through Jesus Christ?

During the days of the Roman emperor Tiberius, Jesus of Nazareth (4–6? B.C.–A.D. ?29–33), a carpenter's adopted son, gained widespread popularity and notoriety in Israel for his authoritative teachings and astounding miracles. The saying spread throughout the region, even among the Gentiles, that Jesus was *Immanuel,* "God with us," the long awaited Christ.

After a brief three- to four-year itinerant ministry, Jesus was condemned by a tribunal of Jewish religious leaders for the blasphemy of claiming to be God's Son and immediately crucified by order of the Roman provincial governor, Pontius Pilate. This fulfilled the Old Testament prophecies foretelling the Messiah's dying agony:

"My heart has turned to wax; it has melted away within me. My strength is dried up like a potsherd, and my tongue sticks to the roof of my mouth; you lay me in the dust of death. Dogs have surrounded me, a band of evil men has encircled me, they have pierced my hands and my feet. I can count all my bones; people stare and gloat over me. They divide my garments among them and cast lots for my clothing" (Psalm 22:14b–18).

"Surely he took our infirmities and carried our sorrows, yet we considered him stricken by God, smitten by him, and afflicted. But he was pierced for our transgressions, he was crushed for our iniquities; the punishment that brought us peace was upon him, and by his wounds we are healed. We all, like sheep, have gone astray, each of us has turned to his own way; and the LORD has laid on him the iniquity of us all" (Isaiah 53:4–6).

According to the Christian Scriptures, known as the New Testament, Jesus Christ was buried late that afternoon, only to rise from the dead three days later. Jesus appeared to more than five hundred followers over the next six weeks and then ascended to heaven from where he had come. Again, this had been prophesied hundreds of years earlier:

"You will not abandon me to the grave, nor will you let your Holy One see decay" (Psalm 16:10).

"[T]hough the LORD makes his life a guilt offering, he will see his offspring and prolong his days, and the will of the LORD will prosper in his hand. After the suffering of his soul, he will see the light of life and be satisfied; by his knowledge my righteous servant will justify many, and he will bear their iniquities" (Isaiah 53:10–11).

First the religious leaders and later the pagan Roman authorities (fiercely after A.D. 60) persecuted the early Christians. The former viewed the Christians as heretics. The latter considered them "atheists" because of their stubborn refusal to worship the lord Caesar or any of Rome's other so-called gods. As a result, many Christian men and women were brutally martyred for their faith.

Despite such severe trials, the early Christians believed their faith presents divine solutions to life's deepest problems. Their teachings come across as surprisingly positive given the fierce hostilities faced by the early Christian apostles and their followers.

From the beginning, Christianity has taken historical facts much more seriously than other wisdom traditions. Its Scriptures were written and rooted in a brief window of Roman history; they abound with historical references to specific cities and caesars, official proclamations and regional famines.

In addition, the Christian Scriptures quote extensively from the Hebrew Bible. In particular, they quote dozens of passages that demonstrate that Jesus, "the son of Abraham, the son of David," is indeed the "Christ," the Anointed One, the promised Messiah.

Early Christianity saw its Scriptures as God's final word to humanity. The closing paragraphs of the New Testament contain a brief warning against adding to or subtracting from anything in its sacred pages:

"I warn everyone who hears the words of the prophecy of this book: If anyone adds anything to them, God will add to him the plagues described in this book. And if anyone takes words away from this book of prophecy, God will take away from him his share in the tree of life and in the holy city, which are described in this book" (Revelation 22:18–19).

Why such severe warning? Like Paul and other apostles, St. Jude spoke of the faith that was "once for all entrusted to the saints" (Jude 3). It wasn't open or subject to further change. In Jesus Christ, God had spoken his final word. Less than two hundred years after the completion of the New Testament, Christians had made a believer of the Roman emperor Constantine, who issued an edict of toleration (A.D. 313) granting Christians the legal freedom to confess Jesus as Lord and worship as they pleased.

Constantine's move may have been politically motivated, yet it demonstrates the remarkable influence and strength of the early Christians. Unfortunately, some of those strengths evaporated with the rapid institutionalization of Christianity.

COMPETING MONOTHEISTIC VISIONS

Monotheistic "holy" wars escalated during the eleventh, twelfth, and thirteenth centuries, when the Church threw its might against the Islamic masses, seeking to take back control of portions of Europe and the Middle East.

Tragically, those crusades ultimately proved more political than spiritual and more bloody than righteous, often at the expense of the Jewish people, as well.

In A.D. 1492, Columbus sailed west across the Atlantic. The terror of the Inquisition reached new heights in Spain and other parts of Europe. Jews and other religious "heretics" were brutally expelled or tortured for their faith; thousands were put to death.

Twenty-five years later, a Catholic monk named Martin Luther challenged the existing hierarchy's abuses of religious (and secular) power by nailing a protest in the form of ninety-five theses on the door of the Wittenberg parish church. From that singular act of defiance (later encouraged by Frederick III, who happened to command the largest army in Europe at the time), the Protestant Reformation began.

As a result of the political/religious tensions created by the Reformation and the ensuing Catholic response, a growing number of prominent European scientists and philosophers began to openly question the need for the Church.

Eventually, *deism*—an abstract belief in a detached Creator God that could do without organized religion, thank you—became popular.

With further advances in the Academy and in association with the Enlightenment, *skepticism* flourished and later an anti-authoritarian *agnosticism* took root.

Within a century, by the 1800s, outright *atheism* became a valid option for a small but growing number of intellectual men and women.

ATHEISM: NO GOD

Widespread atheism is a fairly modern phenomenon, restricted mostly to the past century. With the exception of a few other brave souls, almost no one publicly embraced the idea of going through life alone, defiantly rejecting the idea of God.

The apostles of atheism—Feuerbach, Marx, Nietzsche, and Freud—and others who did espouse atheism were often damning in their criticisms of organized religion.

The eighteenth-century deist Baron d'Holbach said: "It is true, we adore God like ignorant slaves, who tremble under a master whom they know not; we foolishly pray to him, although he is represented to us as immutable; although, in truth, this God is nothing more than nature acting by necessary laws necessarily personified, or destiny, to which the name of God is given."

Sir Julian Huxley stated: "The supernatural is being swept out of the universe. . . . God is beginning to resemble not a ruler, but the last fading smile of a cosmic Cheshire cat."

Before his untimely death, the late Frank Zappa ridiculed the idea of believing in God. The entertainer publicly labeled Christians "the enemy" of his philosophical soulmates, and openly asked believers, "Who you jivin' with that cosmic debris?"

Still others, while not necessarily espousing outright atheism, have been equally damning in their criticisms.

The eighteenth-century Scottish philosopher David Hume, known for his intense skepticism, in his work *Natural History of Religion,* wrote: "Examine the religious principles, which have, in fact, prevailed in the world. You will scarcely be persuaded, that they are other than sick men's dreams."

Oscar Wilde proposed: "Agnosticism should have its ritual no less than faith. It has sown its martyrs, it should reap its saints, and praise God daily for having hidden Himself from man."

American lawyer and writer Clarence Darrow remarked: "I do not pretend to know where many ignorant men are sure—that's all that agnosticism means."

ATHEISM DEFINED

What does *atheism* mean?

Actually, many varieties of atheism abound. Some forms of atheism reject religion. Some reject God. And some say they simply don't want to think about him.

Whatever its slant, every modern form of atheism can be traced back to the landmark writings of Feuerbach, Marx, Nietzsche, and Freud.

American Atheist magazine says, "Atheism may be defined as the mental attitude which unreservedly accepts the supremacy of reason and aims at establishing a lifestyle and ethical outlook verifiable by experience and the scientific method, independent of all arbitrary assumptions of authority and creeds."

Before his disappearance, Jon Garth Murray claimed, "Atheism is a way of life, an entire standard of living centered around trust in oneself and one's own abilities to cope with the pressures of a modern existence."

Holbach referred to an atheist as "a man who destroys the dreams and chimerical beings that are dangerous to the human race so that men can be brought back to nature, to experience, and to reason."

Atheist Ernest Nagel noted that, "historically, atheism has been, and indeed continues to be, a form of social and political protest, directed as much against institutionalized religion as against theistic doctrine."

In *God in Exile,* Cornelio Fabro wrote that "atheism today is coming right out into the open in its operations and organization, with the professed aim of eliminating Christianity as the chief bulwark of resistance. Present-day atheism affirms that man will take possession of his own being to the extent that he expunges from himself and society all awareness of God."

Annie Wood Besant, in *The Gospel of Atheism,* wrote: "The position of the atheist is a clear and reasonable one. I know nothing about God and therefore I do not believe in Him or it. What you tell me about your God is self-contradictory, and is therefore incredible. I do not deny 'God,' which is an unknown tongue to me. I do deny *your* God, who is an impossibility. I am without God."

Gordon Stein, author of *The Encyclopedia of Unbelief,* defines atheism as a "lack of belief in the existence of a God or gods." But "the atheist who denies the existence of God is by far the rarest type of atheist."

To most atheists, then, *God* is a term without meaning. Stein writes: "For unbelievers, the inadequacies in the argument for God's existence indicate that there is no God, that the universe can be explained without reference to God, and that life has to be lived without recourse to God."

According to Stein, atheism clears the mind, increases the ability to reason, and gives each individual full responsibility for his or her actions.

CHANGING TIDE

Down through the ages, humanity has always expressed itself religiously. Only in the twentieth century has any significant percentage of the world's population openly espoused atheistic doctrines.

In 1900, only 0.2 percent of the world's population claimed to be atheistic, agnostic, or nonreligious. By 1990, fully 18.3 percent of humanity, an estimated 988 million people, dismissed God. Furthermore, an estimated one half of the 1.75 billion people who claim affiliation with the world's largest religion weren't sure what they believed about God.

This massive intellectual and religious shift was one of the most striking trends of this past century. Of course, as we saw earlier, that trend has begun to reverse itself.

Robert Frost was right: "Most of the change we think we see in life is due to truths being in and out of favor." Spirituality may be on the upswing now, but that wasn't true only a few short years ago.

Why the dramatic (sometimes Marxist) crusade for antireligion earlier this century? In part, because for the previous three centuries a small handful of self-appointed intellectuals had attacked organized religion with relentless fervor. These writers contradicted the faith of most people, promoting "new truths" under the guise of deeper thinking.

These "truths" appealed to the ego and pride of other aspiring intellectuals, who in turn considered themselves several notches above the "blind" masses. Today, a significant percentage of highly educated individuals believe in God and Jesus Christ. Yet it's sometimes assumed as fact (à la the *Washington Post* several years ago) that someone who says he or she has a personal relationship with God is either ignorant or anti-intellectual. That's ludicrous, of course, as (for instance) the biographies of many of the world's leading scientists demonstrate.

Nevertheless, the seismic shock of out-and-out atheism sent tidal waves of destruction across Europe and beyond, accounting directly for the annihilation and butchering of more than 100 million people this past century alone.

Humanity has paid a steep, gruesome price for the awful experiments in deliberate antitheism carried out by Lenin, Adolf Hitler, Joseph Stalin, Mao Tse-tung, and others—each of whom was profoundly influenced by the writings of the apostles of atheism.

In the next few chapters of Part I, we'll look at the tragic influence and ramifications of their writings, which color the daily experience of so many people, and show why belief in God through Jesus Christ makes more sense now than ever (Part II).

Then (in Part III) we'll explore more deeply the history of the apostles of atheism—Feuerbach, Marx, Nietzsche, Freud—and their predecessors to show how less than a dozen men slowly but successfully warped the concept of "truth" over the course of three centuries.

But, first, I share my son's story . . .

ANDREW'S STORY

Like countless thousands of other people, my son Andrew "lost" any appearance of faith in God during his youth.

Not that Andrew entirely ruined his life. He broke nearly all the rules, yet he was smart enough to draw the line when necessary. Still, his choices, especially at university and afterward, were damaging to himself and others, and grieved his mother and me. We watched a tall, handsome, lovable, and intelligent young man growing increasingly entrenched in a frantic lifestyle, in what appeared to be a futile search for happiness.

At the invitation of Sir Howard Cooke, the Governor-General of Jamaica, and other national leaders, I spent fifteen days traveling throughout that island nation, speaking in stadiums and other venues about God's relevance. Hoping against hope, my wife and I invited Andrew to fly down from Boston to join us for a few days during that speaking tour.

Andrew accepted our invitation, ostensibly to pursue one of his favorite pastimes, fishing. The fishing was fabulous, yet Andrew also made a point of going with us to the Jamaican National Stadium in Kingston where I was finishing the last leg of my speaking tour.

I spoke that night on the rich young ruler who interviewed Jesus yet decided to postpone making a commitment to God (Mark 10:17–22). I had no idea what Andrew thought of my message.

Late that night, long after Patricia and I had gone to bed, Andrew knocked quite vigorously on the door of our hotel room, came in, and told us, in essence, "I've decided to come back home."

Not back to Portland, Oregon, where we live. But back home to God. Soon afterward, following an intense period of "serious repenting," as he calls it, Andrew broke with his loose lifestyle and for the first time embraced true freedom and joy as found in classic, biblical Christianity.

British writer John Hunter once called repentance "the most positive, liberating word in the English language." I now know why.

The past four years, my wife and I, other family members, and Andrew's friends have witnessed an amazing transformation in his life. Rarely have I met someone so sincerely committed to God, so fervently interested in spiritual things, so genuinely happy and at peace, so eager to spread the faith. The glow of his conversion hasn't worn off.

Without "glorying in the past," Andrew readily speaks of his transformation to any and all he meets. Once, after meeting with President Bill Clinton and a small group of religious leaders for breakfast at the White House, I introduced my son to the President. As we talked about the difference God can make in someone's life, Andrew quite naturally shared his story with the President.

The President himself claims to have made a public commitment of faith in God, as a boy, during a Billy Graham evangelistic crusade.

Obviously, everyone's experience is different. What's your story?

Is God relevant to you?

If so, on what basis have you entered into relationship with him?

If not, what has held you back thus far?

CHAPTER 2

IS ANYBODY THERE?

If the apostles of atheism are telling the truth, that God most emphatically is *not* relevant, shall we applaud their insights—or hang our heads in despair?

If Sigmund Freud is right that "God" is an infantile illusion that should be discarded, where does that leave us?

"No one is so much alone in the universe as a denier of God," German writer Jean Paul Richter observed. "With an orphaned heart, which has lost the greatest of fathers, he stands mourning by the immeasurable corpse of the universe."

If Ludwig Feuerbach is right that "God" is a mere projection of our humanity, who is to say we ourselves aren't the figment of someone else's bad dream?

"The absolute death of the word 'God,' including even the eradication of its past, would be the signal, no longer heard by anyone, that man himself had died," theologian Karl Rahner noted.

If Friedrich Nietzsche is right that nihilism is the only way to rightly understand this world, shouldn't we take the first exit out of this miserable and meaningless existence?

"If there is no God, and everything, therefore, is permitted," François Mauriac wrote (echoing a line by Russian novelist Fyodor Dostoevsky), "the first thing permitted is despair."

If Karl Marx is right that the material is all that matters, that there is no heaven or hell, what are we to make of our fragile life on this utterly insignificant and slowly dying planet?

Ask Eric Clapton.

In 1991, Clapton's five-year-old son Conor died after falling out of the window of his mother's New York high-rise. The tragedy inspired Clapton's hit "Tears in Heaven."

Five years later, Clapton opened the front door of his three-story London mansion after a day away and found the inside ablaze. "The first thing I did was grab my guitars," the songwriter told a reporter afterward. "None of them was damaged."

What if Slow Hand hadn't arrived in time? What if all of the rock legend's guitars were destroyed?

According to the apostles of atheism, that event would have been intrinsically equivalent to Clapton's son's death, simply the rearranging of an extremely minute part of this earth's mass into a less complex form.

Granted, Clapton's guitars someday may fetch an incredible sum during an auction held at Sotheby's. But they aren't immortal; only Clapton and Conor and you and me.

Freud claimed that "at bottom no one believes in his own death; or to put the same thing in another way, in the unconscious every one of us is convinced of his own immortality." Yet, like everyone else, Freud too passed away, after a sixteen-year battle with cancer.

Even the most ardent atheist feels death's sting. In a letter to German socialist Ferdinand Lassalle, Marx wrote: "The death of my son has shaken me deeply, and I feel the loss as keenly as though it were only yesterday, and my poor wife has completely broken down under the blow."

Why do we have funerals? To eulogize a loved one, a fellow, a friend. To weep and say goodbye.

If Freud and Marx and Nietzsche and Feuerbach and their followers are right, however, there are no tears in heaven. There is no heaven. Only rearrangements of valueless matter in a mostly empty universe where everything happens by randomness and chance.

Brrrrrrr.

One of this century's most famous atheists, the English mathematician, philosopher, and writer Bertrand Russell—a very outspoken critic of Christian morality and beliefs—conceded that such a materialistic belief system is chilly at best: "There is darkness without and when I die there will be darkness within. There is no splendor, no vastness, anywhere; only triviality for a moment, and then nothing."

Only days before Albert Einstein's death, he and Russell issued a joint statement saying that "those of us who know the most are the gloomiest about the future." Aldous Huxley concurred with them: "Science has 'explained' nothing; the more we know, the more fantastic the world becomes, and the profounder the surrounding darkness."

Double brrrrrrr.

Time essayist Pico Iyer says "a sense of eternity is much less cold and abstract if linked to a sense of divinity." Yet is that option open to us?

Albert Camus called death philosophy's greatest dilemma; "and anyone who has watched a loved one die understands that philosophical problem well," Christian author Ravi Zacharias adds.

George Bernard Shaw once quipped, "The statistics on death are quite impressive. One out of one people die." C. S. Lewis went on to say: "There are, aren't there, only three things we can do about death: to desire it, to fear it, or to ignore it."

Yet ignore death we cannot, especially in today's media-saturated society.

Every day, the media confirm anew that, although people are living twice as long as a century ago, for each of us the end of the world will be the day we die. The Bible says, "Man is appointed to die once, and after that to face judgment" (Hebrews 9:27).

Writing in the aftermath of a horrible air tragedy, *Time* essayist

Lance Morrow observed: "The passengers on Flight 800 began a trajectory to the City of Light and ended, after a few minutes, in a burst, and then the profoundest blackness. An arc of time interrupted by eternity."

The fear of that most terrible of interruptions is real for most people, and for good reason. Even if we live to a ripe old age, in the end Death reaps us all.

One of the richest men in America, Warren Buffett, has made it no secret he fears death above all else. His biographer, Roger Lowenstein, notes: "Warren's exploits were always based on numbers, which he trusted above all else. In contrast, he did not subscribe to his family's religion. Even at a young age, he was too mathematical, and too logical, to make the leap of faith. He adopted his father's ethical underpinnings, but not his belief in an unseen divinity. In a person who is honest in his thoughts, and especially in a boy, such untempered logic can only lead to one terrifying fear—the fear of dying. And Warren was stricken with it." That fear has stayed with him all his life.

Harold Kushner claims: "We are afraid of dying, we cling to life so desperately, not because we enjoy living so much but because we are afraid that this life is all there is. When it is over, it will be truly over. All trace of our existence will disappear. We go to all sorts of extremes to avoid the prospect of disappearing totally after death."

In contrast to such fears, others propose that we should welcome death as a friend. Some go so far as to claim it is the only sure release from the suffering and pain of this mortal existence. If life is hell, and then you die, why not hasten the process?

The atheistic existentialist Jean-Paul Sartre seemed to have thought so, in theory. Yet is suicide really our only option to ongoing philosophical and psychological despair? Obviously not.

If you get cold enough, you could simply grow numb.

Or I could try to deny reality.

Or we could embrace hope.

Is that last option available to us?

Perhaps, if we can convince ourselves that we are not alone in the universe—that God, angels, *someone* is out there. And that he, she, whatever *cares* whether we're here.

ALONE IN THE UNIVERSE?

Arthur C. Clarke, author of *2001: A Space Odyssey,* once said: "Two possibilities exist: either we are alone in the universe or we are not. Both are equally terrifying."

During the writing of this book, the media have had a heyday speculating whether extraterrestrial life may indeed exist, either on Mars or on massive planetlike spheres orbiting around 47 Ursa Major, 51 Pegasi, 70 Virginis, and elsewhere. The national media have been reporting "a new major breakthrough" every few weeks, with more planets discovered in the past year than in the past two millennia.

These breakthroughs have provoked much speculation and breathless announcements from NASA, the media, and leading astronomers. Robert Brown, an astronomer with the Space Telescope Science Institute, declared, "What we are seeing is the culmination of intellectual history that began with Copernicus 500 years ago."

Is anybody out there? The Judeo-Christian Scriptures are emphatic: yes, most definitely. God is out there—and here. Celestial beings, good and evil, are out there—and here. And for more than a century, Christian writers such as George MacDonald, C. S. Lewis, Billy Graham, and others have welcomed the idea that other, mortal forms of extraterrestrial life may exist, as well. If God is God, of course it is conceivable and possible. It is no threat to classic Christian belief.

Still, natural history professor Paul Davies of Australia argues that, if such extraterrestrial life forms exist, they might undermine some aspects of Judeo-Christian theology: ". . . if life on earth is not unique, the case for a miraculous origin would be undermined. The discovery of even a humble bacterium on Mars, if it could be shown to have arisen independently from earth life, would support the view that life emerges naturally."

Davies sets up a false dilemma, however, for nowhere does the Bible say God created life on this planet alone.

As I write this section, the news media have announced the possible discovery of just such a bacterium, based on an analysis of potentially organic molecules discovered in a meteorite found twelve years ago on the icy slopes of the Allan Hills in Antarctica.

Several scientists determined that the meteorite must have originated from Mars, based on comparisons of its chemistry with samples collected during NASA's Viking probes.

Because of the potential ramifications of this discovery that life may have existed on early Mars, NASA administrator Daniel Goldin briefed the President and Vice-President a week before making any public announcements.

Given all the speculation and spending (with NASA asking for much more) in search of signs of extraterrestrial life, a handful of critics have expressed concerns about our priorities.

Who cares about alien life forms? One in two Americans, according to a *Newsweek* poll.

Why should we care? Davies, author of *Are We Alone?* says: "The search for extraterrestrial life is really a search for ourselves—who we are and what our place is in the grand sweep of the cosmos."

He adds: "Bertrand Russell argued that a universe under a death sentence from the second law of thermodynamics rendered human life ultimately futile. All our achievements, all our struggles, 'all the noonday brightness of human genius,' as he put it, would, in the final analysis, count for nothing if the very cosmos itself is doomed.

"Russell's despairing tone is frequently echoed by contemporary thinkers. Thus the French Nobel-prizewinning biologist Jacques Monod writes, 'Man at last knows that he is alone in the unfeeling immensity of the universe, out of which he has emerged only by chance.' "

Davies says, "Traditionally, biologists [over the past century have] believed that life is a freak—the result of a zillion-to-one accidental concatenation of molecules." Fred Hoyle of Cambridge quantified those "zillion-to-one" odds a bit more precisely, putting the figure somewhere near 1×10^{40}. This amazing idea put forth by presumed intellectuals is roughly equivalent to a twister transforming a junkyard into a jumbo jet. Others have compared the odds to an explosion in a print shop producing an unabridged edition of the Oxford Dictionary. In other words, next to impossible.

Yet Davies, like science writer James Trefil and others, argues that some undiscovered law of nature apparently has stacked the odds a bit more favorably *toward* the formation of life. Specifically, Davies hypothesizes, "If matter and energy have an inbuilt tendency to amplify and channel organized complexity, the odds against the formation of life and the subsequent evolution of intelligence could be drastically shortened."

Where this hypothetical "inbuilt tendency" comes from, who knows? But if Davies is right, perhaps the odds are only 1×10^{30}. That still seems to make it statistically improbable that life—a mere bacterium, let alone the likes of you and me—is a "concatenation of molecules."

Unless God is in the picture.

IS GOD THE GREAT DESIGNER, AFTER ALL?

In a National Public Radio interview, Owen Gingerich, professor of astronomy and the history of science at the Harvard-Smithsonian Center for Astrophysics in Cambridge, talked about the implications of our growing understanding of the universe.

First, according to Gingerich, "There are so many wonderful details which, if they were changed only slightly, would make it impossible for us to be here, that one just has to feel, somehow, that there is a design in the universe and, therefore, a designer to have worked it out so magnificently."

Extrapolating the likelihood that even two of those details might be repeated elsewhere in the universe (the right kind of star with a planet exactly the right distance away), in 1966 Carl Sagan and Iosef Shklovskii estimated that 0.001 percent of all known stars might have planets capable of sustaining advanced life forms.

Now, scientists claim a minute change in any one of more than forty observable details, including the sun's luminosity, the earth's surface gravity, or its rotation speed, would obliterate life on this planet. Gingerich argues that those details didn't happen by chance. He sees the hand of God in such incredibly precise design.

Second, according to Gingerich, "we have to come to terms theologically with the notion that we can't limit God's creativity to what is just here on Earth." The incredible vastness of the universe seems to argue against the centrality of history as we know it here on planet Earth. Not only aren't we center stage, we're quite off to one side of the whole show.

For instance, if we could randomly place our most powerful telescopes anywhere else in the universe and look back, probably nine times out of ten it wouldn't be possible to see this planet. Physically, we're infinitesimally small in a finite but immensely large universe.

What about the possibility of finding life on other planets, then? According to Gingerich, "life is, perhaps, easier than we might suppose to get started. On the other hand, the whole notion of intelligent, self-conscious life is another question, and there is a lot of debate on this, and many very distinguished scientists are prepared to argue vehemently that it is so rare that we could have no possible hope of getting in touch with other intelligent life."

Part of the problem gets back to the vastness of the universe. "No one can possibly imagine the dimensions of endless space," outspoken evolutionist Clarence Darrow once claimed. "The great Nebula M.31 in Andromeda is so far away from the earth that it takes light nine hundred thousand millions of years to reach our planet. The nebula itself is so vast that it takes fifty thousand years for light to cross it."

Even though Darrow's figures have proved way off the mark, he still makes the point: "I cannot help feeling sorry for the residents of Nebula M.31 in Andromeda, when I think what a great deprivation they must suffer through living so far away from our glorious planet, which Mark Twain named 'the wart,' but which theology has placed at the centre of the universe and as the sole concern of gods and men."

Traveling at the fantastic velocity of 1.1 million miles an hour, one six-hundredth of the speed of light, it would take nearly five thousand years to travel to the nearest star outside our solar system, Proxima Centauri, and return. To fly to 47 Ursa Major, 51 Pegasi, 70 Virginis, and other stars looking for planets that potentially might sustain observable life forms would take next to forever.

Yet the Scriptures plainly state and history suggests that we are a visited planet. Not by UFOs or aliens, but by divine beings from another dimension, another reality operating beyond the physical limitations that keep us so closely bound to this planet.

Stephen Hawking's and other scientists' hypotheses about ten dimensions of reality collapsing into three during the first infinitesimal fraction of a second of the Big Bang certainly suggest possibilities far beyond the scope of reality we know.

Hoimar von Ditfurth put it this way: "If, from the indubitable fact that the world exists, someone wants to infer a cause of this existence, his inference does not contradict our scientific knowledge at any point. No scientist has at his disposal even a single argument or any kind of fact with which he could oppose such an assumption. This is true, even if the cause—and how could it be otherwise—obviously has to be sought outside this three-dimensional world of ours."

Emil Fackenheim goes so far as to suggest that "the whole battle between science and religion rests on nothing but gigantic misunderstandings on both sides. It was because faith had *already* been undermined by the time this battle was joined in the 19th century, that religion had to resort either to a fundamentalism hostile to all science, or else to a modernism seeking props for its own weaknesses in a science which would not and could not provide them."

That we are indeed a visited planet is what Christmas is all about. Not in the *E.T.* or "X-Files" sense. And not the Christmas of commercialism and consumerism. Instead, I'm speaking of the arrival of God's Son to planet Earth—an event so profound that recorded history is divided before and after its occurrence.

According to *U.S. News & World Report,* sixty-one percent of Americans not only believe in Jesus Christ's first advent, but also believe he will return to earth someday in what is known as the Second Coming.

The New Testament teaches that after Christ's second coming and millennial reign, the eternal state of every man and woman will be pronounced, once and for all. The exclamation point of the final pages of Scripture is that God will dwell with those who love him: "He will wipe every tear from their eyes. There will be no more death or mourning or crying or pain, for the old order of things has passed away" (Revelation 21:4).

If we are not alone in the universe—if God does exist in and far beyond our very limited perceived dimensions of reality—is the option of the hope of heaven open to us?

HOPE BEYOND TOMORROW?

In one of his most famous songs, John Lennon used to urge his listeners to imagine there was no heaven, no hell.

Henry David Thoreau said the same thing a century earlier, claiming we should live "one world at a time" and suggesting it's pure escapism to imagine anything beyond this present life.

For some, the denial of an afterlife has a certain appeal. Billy Graham tells the story of a drunk talking to Robert Ingersoll, the noted antireligionist: "I liked what you said about [the nonexistence of] hell. But, Bob, I want you to be sure about it, because I'm depending on you."

The problem is, how can an agnostic be sure?

On his deathbed, Ingersoll lamented: "Life is a narrow veil between the cold and barren peaks of two eternities. We strive in vain to look beyond the heights. We cry aloud, and the only answer is the echo of our wailing cry." He died quite uncertain of his ultimate destiny.

Interestingly, flipping through the pages of history, I find many individuals feel compelled, at some point, to reject the idea that there might not be a heaven or hell. Plutarch, Heinrich Heine, Miguel de Unamuno, and Dylan Thomas, among others, objected quite strongly to the fatalistic idea of annihilation.

Even Thomas Huxley, who had railed against the idea of an afterlife, wrote this before he died in 1895: "It is a curious thing that I find my dislike to the thought of extinction increasing as I get older and nearer the goal. It flashes across me at all sorts of times and with a sort of horror that in 1900 I shall probably know no more of what is going on than I did in 1800. I had sooner be in hell a good deal—at any rate in one of the upper circles where the climate and company are not too trying."

T. S. Eliot concurred: "I had far rather walk, as I do, in daily terror of eternity, than feel that this was only a children's game in which all the contestants would get equally worthless prizes."

Simone de Beauvoir, companion of Jean-Paul Sartre, believed he was right in saying "Man is alone, abandoned to his own destiny." Yet toward the end of her life she confessed: "I loathe the thought of annihilating myself quite as much now as I ever did."

Even the noted atheist Sir Alfred J. Ayer had second thoughts after a near-death experience.

What's it like "living with Death [the grim reaper] twenty-four hours a day?" *Psycho* author Robert Bloch puts it candidly: "I'm going to die. . . . The problem is, I'm not ready yet. I'm not prepared. . . . I'm frightened [of] what I know and of what I don't know."

Bloch adds: "One thing is already clear—we don't look forward to having him [Death] around. And we'll be anxious for him to depart, except that when he leaves he won't go alone. He won't go alone, but he won't take all of me with him, either. A part will still remain behind, until paper crumbles, film dissolves, and memories fade. Who knows? By the time these things happen, you and I, somewhere or someplace, may meet again. Anyway, it's nice to think so. See you later. I hope."

In *Metamorphosis,* David Suzuki admits: "I have feared death as long as I can remember. As a life-long atheist, I have dreaded, not the process of dying, but the terrible consequence of not *being* forever after."

I do not agree with these men's philosophies, yet I admire their willingness to say what they're thinking. In our postmodern world, few men and women are brave enough to talk openly about their fears of dying or their beliefs about the hereafter. Even when we're actually dying and know we need to talk, we often don't, for fear of offending anyone else's religious beliefs or lack thereof.

Christian writer Philip Yancey notes: "I have been in hospital groups as dying patients worked desperately toward a calm stage of acceptance. Strangely, no one ever talked about heaven in those groups; it seemed embarrassing, somehow cowardly. What convulsion of values can have us holding up the prospect of annihilation as brave and that of blissful eternity as cowardly?"

Not surprisingly, eighty-one percent of Americans believe in heaven, and most think they have a better than average chance of spending eternity there.

Is all that wishful thinking?

Oxford professor C. S. Lewis, who converted from all-out atheism to classic Christianity, argued no: "Heaven is not a state of mind. Heaven is reality itself."

Of course, proponents of half of the wisdom traditions aren't so sure. There's no heaven in Confucianism, Buddhism, or Hinduism. Only the monotheistic religions embrace such hope.

In particular, Jesus Christ spoke often and convincingly of the afterlife. But, some ask, wasn't he simply using figurative language to have a greater moral influence on his listeners?

Boston College philosopher Peter Kreeft says Jesus Christ

"meant to be taken literally when he talked about the existence of heaven and hell. They're real places. We will certainly go to one of them forever. It matters infinitely which. *That* is certainly what he meant everyone to get out of his teaching."

Jesus' disciples obviously got that message, willingly laying down their lives to spread the good news of new, eternal life in Jesus' name. Their utter boldness astounded even Caesar. British Christian writer J. B. Phillips notes: "These early Christians were on fire with the conviction that they had become, through Christ, literally sons of God; they were pioneers of a new humanity, founders of a new Kingdom. . . . Perhaps if we believed what they believed, we might achieve what they achieved."

If in their preaching Jesus and his disciples were serious about the afterlife, if the New Testament truly insists there's a hell to pay, doesn't that cast a dark shadow on God's reputation?

Kreeft argues against the idea of "the badness of God," that he somehow unjustly condemns human beings to an eternity in hell: "Hell is the logical conclusion of sin, of evil." If God created the world, and created man with the free will to rebel against him, then hell follows: we can choose to remain alienated, forever, if we so desire.

G. K. Chesterton put it this way: "Hell is God's great compliment to the reality of human freedom and the dignity of human choice."

"Abandon hope, all ye who enter here," wrote Dante Alighieri in his immortal work, *The Divine Comedy,* quoting an imagined inscription at the entrance to hell. The words startle the imagination. How awful to think of any punishment that continues forever, without hope of relief or reprieve. Yet Dante isn't warning potential victims about to be cast against their will into the fiery inferno.

Instead—and this distinction is important—Dante's scene tells us that only those who abandon all hope in their rebellion against God would even consider venturing into such a hell.

In *People of the Lie,* Scott Peck writes: "God does not punish us; we punish ourselves. Those who are in hell are there by their own choice. . . . Their values are such as to make the path out of hell appear overwhelmingly dangerous, frighteningly painful, and impossibly difficult. So they remain in hell because it seems safe and easy to them. They prefer it that way. This situation and the psychodynamic involved were the subject of C. S. Lewis' fine book *The Great Divorce.* The notion that people are in hell by their own choice is not widely familiar, but the fact is that it is both good psychology and good theology."

Why would anyone volitionally consign himself to unending despair? Lewis put it this way: "The damned are, in one sense, successful rebels to the end; . . . the doors of hell are locked on the inside."

Locked against whom—and why?

God himself—for reasons we shall see.

ROSARIO'S STORY

Rosario was born out of wedlock in the slums outside Lima, Peru. She grew up filled with anger at the lack of food and water and the destitution all around her.

Although she never finished her formal education, Rosario became an avid reader. By age thirteen she was reading Marx and Lenin. By eighteen she had become a militant Communist and atheist.

While training in Cuba, Rosario met famed revolutionary Che Guevara and became his assistant. He filled her with a passion for her country and humanity.

Before Che Guevara went on a mission to Bolivia, he asked Rosario to survey the situation for him. When she warned him not to go, he ignored her advice and met a violent death.

But death was nothing new to Rosario. She hated the upper classes and whoever else stood in her way, and she spilled their blood without remorse during her missions.

Rosario returned to Lima on one particular mission in December 1970. She had become a bitter, angry, calloused woman who hated anything to do with God or Christianity.

When Rosario heard one of my daily Spanish radio programs and found out I would be speaking live at a theater that evening, she became enraged. Even though she didn't know me from Adam, she hated everything I stood for.

During my message I spoke about the "Five Hells of Human Existence"—murder, robbery, deceit, hypocritical homes, and hatred. Each sin I mentioned pricked Rosario's conscience. When I gave the invitation, Rosario came forward with scores of other people. She wasn't thinking of conversion; murder was on her mind. If she had had her gun with her, she would have used it.

An old Christian woman saw Rosario standing there. She went up and said, "Madam, can I help you receive Christ?" Rosario smacked the poor counselor, then panicked at the commotion she caused and ran from the theater.

As Rosario Rivera tossed and turned that night, God impressed two verses from my message on her mind. Jeremiah 17:5 reads, "Cursed is the one who trusts in man, who depends on flesh for his strength and whose heart turns away from the Lord." In contrast, verse 17:7 says, "Blessed is the man who trusts in the Lord, whose confidence is in him."

Very early that morning, Rosario fell on her knees a hardened criminal, and stood back up a child of God. The Lord absolutely revolutionized this Marxist guerrilla, and today she is an amazing testimony to the transforming power of the Word of God.

"If my heart burned for the revolution in the past, then it burns even more now," Rosario said. "And if I did a lot for the poor before, then I do more now." The poor neighborhood where she came from is testimony to this: it and many others now have running water and electric lights, and the good news of Jesus Christ's transforming power, thanks to her efforts.

Chapter 3

HOW DO WE KNOW?

The moment we stop asking questions, we stop thinking.

Walter Savage Landor said, "If there were no falsehood in the world, there would be no doubt; if there were no doubt, there would be no inquiry; if no inquiry, no wisdom, no knowledge, no genius."

In writing this book, my purpose isn't to write an exposé of the apostles of atheism. They're dead and gone. Instead, as stated in the Introduction, my aim is to help readers explore some of the prevalent atheistic postmodern prejudices and then examine whether those prejudices make sense.

Is it possible that you and I are more than minute and accidental concatenations of matter lost in the vast cosmos, without known origin, identity, meaning, or purpose?

Is it even possible to address such questions if God isn't in the picture?

ASKING THE RIGHT QUESTIONS

In her books about alleged past lives, actress Shirley MacLaine claims her beliefs "are all concerned with ancient questions. Why are we here? Where did we come from? Is there a God?" To her credit, MacLaine is asking the right questions, questions philosophers have been asking since antiquity.

Many disagree with MacLaine, however, about how best to answer those same questions. One of this world's most successful actresses will fail for words someday, in another world. Tears alone will not endear her to her Maker. God already loves her and longs for relationship with her, yet for years she has rejected him out of hand.

It isn't enough to ask the right questions, as important as that is. Ultimately, life is about discovering and embracing good and right answers. Not "perfect" answers, of course, because who has a corner on the truth? Only Jesus Christ, who is truth personified (John 14:6). Only Jesus points the way to God, to ultimate reality.

Outside God and his revelation in the Scriptures, we're lost. Claiming "We long to see the orphan file," the late Carl Sagan described humans as newborn babies left on Earth's doorstep with no note explaining who we are and where we came from, let alone where we go from here.

Religious writer W. Ward Gasque said, "Modern man has scarcely any idea how to begin to answer these questions. As a result, in the words of the philosopher Nicholas Berdyaev, he 'lives in agony.' Having given up faith in God, he finds that he no longer has faith in man, least of all in himself."

Gasque goes on to say: "Among intellectuals, this present predicament of man has led many to despair, 'to writhe in the convulsions of the catastrophe called Nihilism' (as Nietzsche predicted). In general society, the loss of a sense of purpose in life has led people to seek consolation in a relentless and never-to-be-satisfied 'pursuit of happiness' fraudulently promised by the American Declaration of Independence as man's inalienable right, and by means of the frantic pursuit to avoid the hard questions about existence. But the questions won't go away."

RECURRING QUESTIONS

The questions keep coming back to us as we read, listen to the radio, watch television, and surf the Net. Even Hollywood keeps bringing them up.

In *Groundhog Day,* for instance, Bill Murray plays ambitious, egotistical Pittsburgh television weatherman Phil Connors, who, against his wishes, travels to the little hamlet of Punxsutawney to report on the annual groundhog festival. It's his fourth—"and last"—trip to Punxsutawney, Phil tells his producer (Andie MacDowell). He's ready for the big time, and feels this little story is quite beneath a weatherman of his caliber.

Ironically, despite Phil's confident predictions the night before, a blizzard hits just outside Punxsutawney immediately after the festival. Phil, his producer, and the cameraman are stuck overnight in the tiny hamlet.

The only problem is, when Phil Connors wakes up the next morning, it's not the next morning—it's February 2 all over again. He's worried—very worried something has gone wrong with his head. It's déjà vu—all day long.

Worse, the *next* morning—it's Groundhog Day, take three. Phil Connors starts losing it, bad, until it occurs to him that he can do anything he wants if there is no tomorrow. He drinks like a slob, robs an armored truck for more cash, picks up women left and right, and treats most people with utter contempt. Living a life of license, he becomes the worst of persons.

Phil eventually becomes so disgusted with himself and his hopeless situation that he commits suicide—only to wake up and do Groundhog Day all over again. He immediately goes out and kills himself again—but nothing, no matter how dramatic, works. He's stuck on February 2, forever. He keeps changing, but everything else stays the same.

Accepting his immortality, Phil finally confides to his producer over breakfast, "I'm a god." Of course, to her this is *the* Groundhog Day—she doesn't know what he's talking about.

"I'm an immortal," he explains. "I want you to believe in me." She's skeptical, to say the least.

"How do you know I'm not a god?" Phil asks. He then goes on to prove he knows everything about everyone in the café—who they are, what they're going to do that day, even what they're going to say next.

"I know everything," Phil brags.

Shortly thereafter he says, "I've killed myself so many times I don't even exist anymore."

Phil then goes into a self-improvement kick. Through a seemingly endless cycle of Groundhog Days, he masters the piano, French poetry, medicine, even ice sculpturing. With practice, he's always at the right spot at the right time to catch a boy falling out of a tree, save a homeless man dying on a cold winter night, give the Heimlich maneuver to a man choking in a restaurant, change the tire for an old lady who just got a flat. You name it—it's Phil to the rescue. By day's end, Phil is a celebrity in ole Punxsutawney.

The next day, it's the same routine all over again, only this time a little better.

At one point, Phil wonders out loud if this is how God does what he does. If not, how *does* he do it all?

Finally it happens—the producer spends the night with Phil at a cozy bed and breakfast (no, nothing happens in bed). The next morning it's February 3, at last. The spell is broken, and Phil can go on with his life—a much better man.

The movie has all the makings of a classic—humorous, tragic, philosophical, romantic. The main character is redeemed, the credits roll, and we're left wondering, "Now what was that all about, really?"

It's intriguing to watch this movie, not for any answers, but to see so many big questions raised in such a short period of time. Depending on your belief system, you could say it argues for atheism or agnosticism, for Buddhism or Hinduism, even for Christianity. Why? Because it teaches any of those religious (or antireligious) belief systems? No. Simply because it raises the right kinds of questions.

DOES ANYONE KNOW THE RIGHT ANSWERS?

My point is this: asking the right questions only proves we're starting to think along some very big, important lines.

Unless you and I know good answers to questions like "Who am I?" and "Where did I come from?" however, how can we even begin to address questions like "Where am I going?" and "How am I going to get there?" and "What should I expect?" and "Who might be awaiting me?" and "Why should I care?"

In this book, I'm inviting you to think some big thoughts along with me and see where they lead. My conclusion, of course, is that God is relevant, and that you can experience this for yourself by opening the door of your heart to Jesus Christ.

If at any point you think I'm getting off track, please, disagree with me. Take out your pen and write specific objections or counterarguments at the end of each chapter. Thoroughly mark up each section—underline key points, scribble exclamation points and question marks in the margins, cross out whole pages if you must.

This is your book—you can make of it whatever you want. Some readers may come to a point of faith in God through Jesus Christ; others will put it aside in disbelief and say, "See, I told you so."

I often find those most argumentative about God's relevancy are actually the closest to embracing faith. Those who say, "Sure, everyone knows that," sometimes are the furthest from wanting to experience God's presence or power in their lives.

Over the years, I've had the privilege of living in four countries and logging millions of miles, making friends in more than sixty nations. I've spent well over half of my life overseas. My wife and I circle the globe two or three times each year.

In my travels, I've had the opportunity to become friends with presidents, prime ministers, members of royalty, ambassadors, governors, mayors. With college professors, executives of Fortune 500 companies, media managers, and journalists. And with professional athletes, entrepreneurs, entertainers, and university students.

Everywhere I go, everyone I meet, I find that people want to know, Is God relevant? If so, how is God relevant? How can I know him? And will knowing God through Jesus Christ make a difference?

While in Scotland in 1980, my wife discovered a lump. We immediately returned home to the United States and went to see Patricia's physician. For a moment we sat in stunned silence, trying to block out his awful words: "The tumor is malignant and radical surgery must be performed immediately. We can't delay." Surgery was scheduled for the following Monday. Pat had cancer.

When we arrived home, I headed for the basement to sit in my office. Somehow I had to come to grips with this terrible news. A hundred emotions welled up inside of me and I started to cry. This was the sort of thing that happened to other people. But not to my wife. Not to Pat.

My thoughts were suddenly interrupted by the strains of a familiar old Christian hymn. Where was it coming from? My four sons were all at school. No one was in the house except Pat and me. Slowly it dawned on me—Pat herself was playing the piano and singing, "How firm a foundation, ye saints of the Lord / Is laid for your faith in His excellent Word: / What more can He say than to you He hath said, / to you who for refuge to Jesus have fled?"

When the bottom seemed to be falling out of our lives, my wife found strength and peace in the firm foundation of her relationship with Jesus Christ. She had trusted Christ as a girl, confirmed her faith through the years, and distinctly grown in her relationship with God.

What if we hadn't believed in God? At the time, a significant percentage of breast cancer patients died as a result of that horrible, cruel disease. If we angrily dismissed God out of hand, where would we have turned for encouragement and hope?

Only in the Scriptures did Patricia find the comfort and solace she needed. Thankfully, that was exactly what some of her closest friends shared with her in that great time of need. Verses such as:

" 'For I know the plans I have for you,' declares the LORD, 'plans to prosper you and not to harm you, plans to give you hope and a future' " (Jeremiah 29:11).

" 'Surely I will be with you always, to the very end of the age' " (Matthew 28:20b).

"Cast all your anxiety on him [God] because he cares for you" (1 Peter 5:7).

I'll admit, I disagree with many of the presuppositions and beliefs of my atheistic friends and acquaintances. More than a few are unafraid to strongly disagree with me. But at least one has admitted I have the edge over him in this: when Patricia's cancer went into remission, we could thank God with all our hearts. When something truly good happens to my friend, he doesn't know whom to thank.

That doesn't mean questions don't come my way. Over the years, however, I've come to the place where I no longer have doubts. As Landor said, without doubts who would ask the tough questions, let alone strive to embrace solid answers? Thankfully, there are solid answers to embrace.

Christian author Paul Little wrote: "Doubt and questioning are normal to any thinking person. It is important, however, that we never equate our lack of an answer to a particular question with the nonexistence of an answer."

ANSWERS, ANYONE?

Students taking their final psychology exam at a major American university worried about which detailed questions might appear on the exam. Those fears quickly dissipated when the professor pointed to the blackboard, announced, "That's the exam," and promised to return in two hours. On the blackboard appeared a single question.

"Why?"

The psychology students feverishly attempted to write extended answers to that short but immense question. In the end, however, only one student passed the exam. At the top of his paper, he had written his name and this reply:

"Why not?"

Sometimes, God alone knows the answers to the really big questions.

According to *Time*, "To the ultimate question—what existed before the big bang—most of modern science is mute."

Nearly thirty-five hundred years ago, Moses reminded the Israelites, "The secret things belong to the LORD our God, but the things revealed belong to us and to our children forever" (Deuteronomy 29:29).

If the Scriptures indeed contain God's revelation to humanity, which I believe is precisely the case, that's significant. If from those truths we can learn how God can become relevant to ourselves and our families, there is hope after all.

Hope that our existence has meaning, purpose, significance. Hope that fulfills our most pressing needs. Hope that overcomes our greatest fears.

That is if, as we inquire further, we can truly overcome the postmodern prejudices instilled in us by the apostles of atheism and their hopelessness, pessimism, skepticism, anger, guilt, and despair.

MARK'S STORY

Is God relevant to life's toughest questions? Just ask Mark, a police officer.

"At age twenty-five, my heart already was fairly hardened. I knew something was missing in my life, so I had looked first to rock music, idolizing some of its heroes. That left me empty. I then looked to alcohol and relationships, then went along the intellectual route and studied psychology and human behavior at university.

"After university, I joined the police force looking for answers, but soon realized that my job dealt with the effects of people's problems, and not the causes. None of these areas provided the answer—something was definitely missing.

"When I had looked at religion and the Church it seemed dull, empty, boring, and irrelevant, but when my wife asked me to accompany her to see Luis Palau, he gave me an answer I had not considered . . . Jesus Christ.

"From the moment Luis Palau rose to his feet, my attention was fixed and I listened with one hundred percent concentration. As he spoke I realized that the words he was speaking were from God and God was speaking to me.

"For the first time I understood why Jesus had died for me. I became aware of God's tremendous love for me. When I heard about receiving God's forgiveness, knowing his love and being able to know him personally on a day-to-day basis, and then being told of the promise of eternal life, I remember thinking, 'What a great idea, but what's the catch?' and the Lord saying to my heart, 'There's no catch, that's the deal.'

"Everything then seemed very straightforward. I realized what had been missing in my life—the Lord Jesus Christ. I then made the most important decision of my life—I stopped going my own way, asked the Lord's forgiveness, and accepted Jesus as Lord and Savior. I remember thinking as I drove home, 'Why has nobody told me this before?'

"Within a few months, my wife's sister and brother and my sister also became Christians and, following this, my wife's sister-in-law and my brother-in-law. This had a domino effect across four separate families with other members subsequently becoming Christians.

"The Lord has helped me in many ways since my conversion. In my job in the police force it was great to have the peace and security of knowing that he was with me every minute of every tour of duty, especially in the more dangerous and tricky moments.

"In my marriage, the Lord has greatly helped and has strengthened my relationship with my wife considerably and has blessed us with three children."

The legacy Mark will leave to his family, for generations to come, reminds me of the words of Patrick Henry, in his will: "I have now disposed of all my property to my family. There is one thing more I wish I could give them, and that is faith in Jesus Christ. If they had that and I had not given them one shilling, they would be rich; and if I had not given them that, and had given them all the world, they would be poor indeed."

What about your own family and circle of friends?

What will be your legacy?

Have you given them encouragement to trust God?

CHAPTER 4

THE (WHOLE) TRUTH?

If the apostles of atheism and their soul mates are right, science and truth are on their side. Are they?

As we'll see further in Part III, the founding father of modern atheism, Ludwig Feuerbach, actively promoted atheism by claiming he had "modern science" on his side and saying he was promoting "the science of reality in its truth and totality."

Friedrich Nietzsche converted to atheism after reading German theologian David Friedrich Strauss's supposedly scientific-literary theories about the New Testament accounts of the life and ministry of Jesus Christ.

Another contemporary in the mid-nineteenth century said Strauss was one of the few men to understand the "unavoidable conflict between the discredited, dominant doctrines of Christianity and the illuminating, rational revelation of modern science."

Going beyond Charles Darwin, German philosopher and naturalist Ernst Haeckel completely rejected the divine: "There are no gods or goddesses, assuming that god means a personal, extramundane entity. This 'godless world-system' substantially agrees with the monism or pantheism of the modern scientist."

In turn, Haeckel quoted from philosopher Arthur Schopenhauer with approval: "Pantheism is only a polite form of atheism. The truth of pantheism lies in its destruction of the dualist antithesis of God and the world, in its recognition that the world exists in virtue of its own inherent forces."

Renouncing religion as an infantile illusion, Sigmund Freud advocated that his followers venture into "hostile life and strive for a new religion through science," which has "given us evidence by its numerous and important successes that it is no illusion."

In seeking to assert "truth," each of these atheists objected strongly to both God and the Scriptures. Shall we follow suit?

SCIENCE VS. GOD?

Many scientists today have no idea what such loud protests against God and the Bible are about. During the past two generations a significant number have openly stated that they adhere to one (or several) of the wisdom traditions.

In particular, many eminent scientists have publicly acknowledged a belief in God: Robert Jastrow (founder of NASA's Goddard Institute of Space Studies), Gerhard Dirks (who helped develop the IBM memory system), Henry F. Schaefer III (nominated for the Nobel prize in chemistry), Sir John Eccles (Nobel laureate and internationally renowned neurobiologist), Chandra Wickramasinghe (with Sir Fred Hoyle described as "two of Britain's most eminent scientists"), Sir Alexander Fleming (the discoverer of penicillin), Lord Ernest Rutherford (of Cambridge, under whose leadership the atom was first split), Sir Robert Boyd (former professor of physics at the University of London), John Houghton (former professor of astrospheric physics at Oxford University), Rupert Sheldrake (former director of biochemistry at Cambridge), Henry Margenau (Yale professor of physics for more than forty years), Robert Griffiths (Carnegie-Mellon professor of mathematical physics), Owen Gingerich (Harvard-Smithsonian astrophysicist), Bob Kaita (Princeton physicist), John Suppe (Princeton geologist), Raymond Damadian (inventor of MRI), and many, many others.

Jastrow, for one, said his colleagues were caught off guard by their discoveries about the origins of the universe: "The scientist's pursuit of the past ends at the moment of creation. This is an exceedingly strange development, unexpected by all but the theologians."

He added: "It is not a matter of another year, another decade of work, another measurement, or another theory; at this moment it seems as though science will never be able to raise the curtain on the mystery of creation. For the scientist who has lived by his faith in the power of reason, the story ends like a bad dream. He has scaled the mountains of ignorance; he is about to conquer the highest peak; as he pulls himself over the final rock, he is greeted by a band of theologians who have been sitting there for centuries."

In other words, science and religion aren't inevitably or always in conflict. Eccles is more pointed: "We need to discredit the belief . . . that science will ultimately deliver the final truth about everything. . . . Science has gone too far in breaking down man's belief in his spiritual greatness and has given him the belief that he is merely an insignificant animal who has arisen by chance."

Yale's Margenau added that "if you take the outstanding physicists, the ones who have done the most to advance modern physics, especially Heisenberg, Schroedinger, Dirac (a Nobel Prize winner), you find them all interested in religion. All these men were intensely interested in religion."

This religious dedication was shared by many of the greatest scientists of the past, including Galileo Galilei ("As to the truth, of which mathematical demonstrations give us the knowledge, it is the same which the Divine Wisdom knoweth"), Johannes Kepler ("God wanted us to recognize those laws by creating us after his own image so that we could share in his own thoughts"), Isaac Newton ("This most beautiful system of the sun, planets and comets, could only proceed from the counsel and dominion of an intelligent and powerful Being"), Robert Boyle (who said much about religion in his scientific writings), and Louis Pasteur (who devoted his scientific work to God's glory).

MODERN SCIENCE AND CHRISTIANITY

British writer A. N. Triton describes the rise of modern science as a product of Protestant Christian thought, adding that "there are plenty of philosophers of science who have pointed out that it was not until certain specifically Christian attitudes were added to the background of pre-Christian philosophy that science as we know it really got under way."

Philosopher Alfred North Whitehead concurred: "Without this belief [in God's creation of man and nature], the incredible labors of scientists would be without hope. It is . . . the motive power of research—that there is a secret, a secret which can be revealed. . . . It must come from the medieval insistence on the rationality of God, conceived as with the personal energy of Jehovah [YHWH] and with the rationality of a Greek philosopher. Every detail was supervised and ordered: the search into nature could only result in the vindication of the faith of rationality."

Echoing Whitehead, Emil Fackenheim agreed that the Christian (specifically Protestant) world view "made modern experimental science possible. Hence one might well conclude that in some ways modern science is closer in spirit to Biblical faith than its pre-modern predecessor." Why? Because the biblical world view sees nature as "the *work* of God," not something "shot through with divinity."

The late professor John H. Gerstner went so far as to say: "True science is suckled at the breast of faith [in God], takes its first step holding the hand of faith, walks by faith, and arrives at a goal of faith."

Physicist Freeman Dyson said the ultimate challenge he and his fellow scientists face "is to try to formulate some statement of the ultimate purpose of the universe. In other words, the problem is to read the mind of God."

Time essayist Dennis Overbye notes, however: "There is no reason to think we even know the right questions yet, let alone ultimate answers. The currency of science is not truth but doubt.

"And, paradoxically, faith. Science is nothing if not a spiritual undertaking. The idea that nature forms some sort of coherent whole, a universe, ruled by laws accessible to us, is a faith. The creation and end of the universe are theological notions, not astronomical ones."

Thankfully, the mind of God, in so far as he wants us to know it, is revealed in nature, Jesus Christ, and the pages of Scripture. Oxford professor C. S. Lewis stated: "In science we have been reading only the notes to a poem; in Christianity we find the poem itself."

WHAT "SCIENCE"?

Ironically, many people still think an appeal to "science" is a damning argument against God's existence and the relevance of his word. "Science" is an intimidating club when wielded in an argument, to be sure. Unless, that is, someone has the presence of mind to ask, "What do you mean by 'science'?"

If by "science" someone means the sum total of humanity's current knowledge and wisdom, she is using a hopelessly general and broad definition. If by "science" someone means the latest ideas expounded by the media, he is simply repeating hypotheses, at best.

To ensure we are making sense, let's define several terms.

A specific definition of *science* is "knowledge of the physical world as obtained and tested by the scientific method," to be distinguished from hypotheses or theories, ideas that are still being tested.

The *scientific method* includes "principles and procedures for the systematic pursuit of knowledge of the physical world, specifically involving (a) the recognition and formulation of a problem, (b) the survey of hypotheses, (c) the collection of relevant data through observation and experimentation, and (d) the testing of hypotheses."

A *scientist,* then, is "one who uses the scientific method to gain knowledge of the physical world."

Science, however, is not to be confused with scientism. *Scientism* is "an exaggerated trust in the efficacy of the scientific method to (a) explain social, psychological, or religious phenomena, (b) solve pressing human problems, or (c) provide a comprehensive unified picture of the meaning of the cosmos." Scientism is scientific pride gone beserk.

For the record, the apostles of atheism were not scientists, nor the sons of scientists. Rather, as their own writings suggest, Feuerbach, Freud, and the rest were high on scientism.

Gerstner wrote convincingly against the dubious idea that only what can be tested by the senses is real. He noted that "science tends toward faith and not away from it provided we avoid scientism, which denies too much because it knows too little."

Gerstner goes on to say that even "the most exact of all the sciences, mathematics, is most clearly based on faith. Have you ever seen a mathematical dot, which is a point without dimension? Have you ever seen a mathematical line, which is length without thickness? Have you ever seen a mathematical square, which possesses length and width but no depth? To be sure, we may conceive what we cannot visualize, but so soon as that distinction is recognized, we are inoculated against scientism."

It's mostly nonscientists, unaware of the limitations of science, who imbibe scientism.

Still, because of the attacks they've received at the hands of some religionists, a number of scientists are justifiably leery of the monotheistic wisdom traditions.

Steven Weinberg, professor of physics and astronomy at the University of Texas in Austin, for instance, takes the fact that religion has been "a traditional source of hostility to science" as sufficient reason to keep his distance.

Noted church historian Martin Marty observes, however, that most religions today are "theologically open to all kinds of science." Still, Weinberg, like many others within the Academy, worries that religion "doesn't care to argue for the truth of anything."

What kind of "truth" is he talking about?

VARIETIES OF TRUTH?

Michael Scriven argues that "the idea of separating religious from scientific knowledge and making each an independent realm with its own basis in experience of quite different kinds is a counsel of despair."

I'm not advocating a two-tiered view of reality. Yet most of life goes beyond mere scientific knowledge.

Scientism deals with the *material* only.

Most of life deals with *relationships*—with God, with one's parents, with one's siblings, with one's spouse, with one's ex, with one's children, grandchildren, relatives, friends, neighbors, associates, and acquaintances in cyberspace.

Life is about honesty and justice, and about love between friends, family, husband and wife, and God. Life is about joy. It's about peace. It's about finding strength from God to face the storms of life.

Religious "truths" aren't verifiable by sense data alone. That certainly doesn't mean I don't care about the truth of what I believe. It's just that most truths—and certainly the most important truths—are found outside the laboratory. Family, friends, ministers, mentors, writers, reporters, historians, and others all strive to fill in the gaps of our knowledge where scientists—by definition—can't help us.

Stanford University professor Richard H. Bube noted almost twenty-five years ago: "One of the most pernicious falsehoods ever to be almost universally accepted is that the scientific method is the only reliable way to truth." Still, the myth persists.

Which men and women have made the most significant contributions to contemporary culture, good or bad? Which forms of government are best and worst suited for the various former Soviet republics? What are the most and least effective means to reduce substance abuse among thirteen- to fifteen-year-old young women? What are the most helpful and harmful ways to cultivate a rich spiritual heritage for my children and grandchildren? Science can't tell us. It shouldn't even try.

Science can no more tell you and me how to live our lives than it can prove exactly what we had for breakfast the day before yesterday. That doesn't mean science isn't important. We all benefit from its advances, in many ways, every day. But when Joseph Stalin, at the dawn of the atomic age, proclaimed, "Science is the savior of mankind," and when Freud ridiculed the idea of Christian salvation while singing the praises of Communism's "promise of a better future," they were dead wrong. *Scientism* is a fatally flawed atheistic faith in humanity's current grasp and use of materialistic knowledge. It's a false use of good science. It's an attempt by those who hold an atheistic faith to use science to deny the existence and relevance of God.

When it comes to matters of faith, Carl Sagan and other atheistic scientists often have overextended themselves. To imply that God doesn't exist because they can't find him when they look in their microscopes or telescopes is illogical. It is insulting to a serious, honest thinker

Paul Little put it well: "To insist that God be 'proved' by the scientific method is like insisting that a telephone be used to measure radioactivity. It simply wasn't made for that."

Yet just because God is beyond the material doesn't mean he has no part in it.

CARICATURES OF SCIENCE?

It's said that when French mathematical physicist Pierre Simon de Laplace presented his first volume on celestial mechanics to Napoleon, the emperor thumbed through the work, then asked whether God played any role in his analysis of the solar system.

"Sire, I have no need of that hypothesis," Laplace replied. Why? He had worked out the problems of Newton's *Celestial Mechanics,* he thought, making any references to what God supposedly had to do (every few years) to keep Jupiter in orbit around the sun no longer necessary.

Laplace later seemed to back away from the suggestion that he had proved God isn't the Creator and Governor of the universe. Scientists today actually need God more than ever.

Still, scientists need not make *God* part of their materialistic hypotheses, any more than they need to put *themselves* into their hypotheses. Physicists Werner Heisenberg and Dietrich Schroeer and Harvard biologist-historian Everett J. Mendelsohn, among others, however, have contended that taking everyone out of the picture isn't always easy. Why? In part, because scientists don't check their presuppositions at the door, because the very act of observing disrupts some aspect of nature, and because many hypotheses have dramatic implications.

As I write this chapter, a team of British scientists has announced it may have found evidences of life in another meteorite from Mars. (If their hypothesis proves true, it simply reinforces what I, as a Christian, believe about God as the Creator of the universe and certainly doesn't take away at all from the role of Jesus Christ as Savior.)

Unfortunately, a few media reports left out the "hypothesis" part of the story, reporting the scientists' findings as already established fact. Scientifically, that's going too far, too fast, violating journalism's standards of excellence and misleading the general public.

Sir Robert Boyd, emeritus professor of physics in the University of London, lamented that at times "we are subjected by the media to a caricature of science which uses its authority to pronounce where its writ does not run."

In a telling commentary, Paul Raeburn, *Business Week*'s senior editor for science and technology, discusses the problems of what he titles "Junk Science and Mass Hysteria." He cites the mad cow disease crisis, Advil's ad campaign about the possible risks associated with high intake of both Tylenol and alcohol, and the long-running dispute over the safety of silicone breast implants as examples.

Such crises occur, Raeburn contends, when a "complex scientific debate is suddenly thrust upon an anxious public that is ill-equipped to understand it." Pandemonium prevails for years, sometimes, until the core of real science gets sorted out.

Raeburn states: "Unresolved scientific disputes have become a fact of modern life. Nothing else so clearly illustrates science's limits."

DOES SCIENCE KNOW ALL?

The apostles of atheism and some of their followers talk as if science is God and scientists are true religion's high priests—as if science knows all and can do all. Not quite!

Most scientists are among the first to acknowledge science's limits. The noted biologist Jacob von Uexküll admitted: "No one of us knows what life is." French physicist Louis Victor de Broglie, a brilliant theoretician concerning problems of light, wrote: "How much we would know if we knew what a ray of light is." A Stanford University scientist told me, "Electricity in its essence is quite unexplainable."

Even what we do know is far from complete. Take the experience of the English physicist Lord John William Strutt Rayleigh and English chemist Sir William Ramsay, for instance. Using different methods, both isolated nitrogen, although they came up with slightly different results when measuring nitrogen's atomic weight. They accepted each other's findings as correct, without minimizing the differences. The discovery of argon, another element, later explained the discrepancy between these two men's research.

Even though a limited number of apparent disagreements exist between religion and science, Albert Einstein (for one) insisted such differences don't negate humanity's earnest efforts to understand either the material or the supramaterial. The celebrated physicist observed: "What is the meaning of human life, or of organic life altogether? To answer the question at all implies religion. Is there any sense, then, you ask, in putting it? I answer, the man who regards his own life and that of his fellow-creatures as meaningless is not merely unfortunate but almost disqualified for life."

Einstein also wrote: "Most people say that it is the intellect which makes a great scientist. They are wrong; it is the character." It's not possible to be *only* a scientist, any more than it's possible to be *only* rational.

This physicist described himself as "a deeply religious man," like many other great physicists of his generation. His religious concepts were shaped by Schopenhauer and seventeenth-century Dutch philosopher Baruch Spinoza, however, not by biblical Judaism or Christianity.

Einstein claimed that "cosmic religious feeling" was his "strongest and noblest incitement to scientific research." He saw no conflict between celebrating such feelings and doing without dogma, church, or priest.

He explained: "My religion consists of a humble admiration of the illimitable superior Spirit who reveals Himself in the slight details we are able to perceive with our frail and feeble minds. That deeply emotional conviction of the presence of a superior reasoning power, which is revealed in the incomprehensible universe, forms my idea of God."

Why didn't Einstein embrace traditional religion? Charles Misner, a scientific specialist in general relativity theory, suggests: "He must have looked at what the preachers said about God and felt that they were blaspheming. He had seen much more majesty than they had ever imagined, and they were just not talking about the real thing. My guess is that he simply felt that religions he's run across did not have proper respect . . . for the author of the universe."

Einstein had started out an atheist. By 1929, however, astronomer Edwin Hubble's work forced Einstein to abandon his "repulsive force" hypothesis and acknowledge "the necessity of a beginning" and "the presence of a superior reasoning power."

For Einstein, it was enough to think of God as "a pure mathematical mind," the essence behind the all-important law of causality, which he practically worshiped.

Einstein's faith didn't go far enough: he missed the point that God is both the Creator and Governor of the universe. The Bible declares:

"In the beginning, God created the heavens and the earth" (Genesis 1:1).

"By faith we understand that the universe was formed at God's command, so that what is seen was not made out of what was visible" (Hebrews 11:2).

"Lift your eyes and look to the heavens. Who created all these? He who brings out the starry host one by one, and calls them each by name. Because of his great power and mighty strength, not one of them is missing" (Isaiah 40:26).

Even though Einstein contributed to the development of quantum theory, its statistical uncertainty struck him as somehow wrong. "Quantum mechanics is certainly imposing," Einstein admitted. "But an inner voice tells me it is not yet the real thing. The theory says a lot, but does not really bring us any closer to the secret of the 'old one.' I, at any rate, am convinced that He is not playing at dice."

Again, "We have become Antipodean in our scientific expectations. You believe in a God who plays dice, and I in complete law and order in a world which objectively exists, and which I, in a wildly speculative way, am trying to capture."

Instead, quantum theory captured the day. Its uncertainty factor provoked much speculation about whether "truth" is relative. According to Alan Harrington, in *Life in the Crystal Palace*, in the marketplace (and elsewhere) that idea has won the day: truth claims are based on what one's superior says, not ascertainable reality.

Harrington says: "It is one of the most characteristic and destructive developments of our own society that man, becoming more and more of an instrument, transforms reality more and more into something relative to his own interests and functions."

"Truth" has become relative not only in the marketplace but also in the Academy, the political arena, and other spheres of life. Other "values" shape what we say and how we say it: to some degree, we're all spin masters, serving vested interests.

So are the Hindus right, after all, that one's interpretations of reality are just as valid as someone else's opposing views? According to pollster George Barna, seventy-two percent of Americans now say yes.

Even half the people in church last weekend have the feeling that truth is relative. Yet that's contrary to the teachings of Scripture and to reality. After all, truth is "actual objects, events, facts, statements, and propositions," without distortion, misrepresentation, or falsehood.

When everyone does what is right in his or her own eyes, regardless of truth, moral chaos and immense social problems invariably follow. We've certainly seen that in America in this past generation, as William Bennett and others have documented.

The answer isn't a "Christian" President or "Christian" laws, but personal conversion to God through Jesus Christ, who is "the way and the truth and the life" (John 14:6).

IS CHRISTIANITY TOO EXCLUSIVE?

In our syncretistic society, it sometimes surprises people that conversion Christianity teaches that individuals are free to reject its truth claims.

Classic Christianity recognizes that the peoples of this world may choose to worship a host of gods or no gods at all. It doesn't seek to obliterate those who disbelieve the Lord God, but seeks rather to win them over with its good news of salvation—a message based on actual, verifiable historical facts.

Philosopher Mortimer Adler says, "Christianity is the only world religion that is evangelical in the sense of sharing good news with others. Islam converts by force; Buddhism, without the benefit of a theology; Hinduism doesn't even try."

Still, good news is only good if it's believed and received. The late theologian Francis Schaeffer spoke of "taking the roof off" postmodern beliefs by exposing their fallacies and then presenting the historical truth content of classic Christianity. The problem? If someone doesn't embrace belief in God, he or she may *feel* worse off than before.

Even embracing faith in God is no guarantee of bliss. C. S. Lewis said, "If you want a religion to make you feel really comfortable, I certainly don't recommend Christianity."

Italian theologian Domenico Grasso wrote about the need to have "the courage to tell listeners the truth. This is not an easy task because nobody likes to say what displeases others. But it is necessary and it demands faithfulness to one's mission."

Why the need for courage?

Writer Don Marquis said it well: "If you want people to think they're thinking, they'll love you: but if you really make them think, they'll hate you."

Yet Peter Kreeft asks: "Would you rather believe a lie that made you happy or the truth even if it made you unhappy?"

Kreeft laments the fact that modern philosophers, psychologists, and others "design complexities to avoid uncomfortable simplicities" and encourage people "to believe things for a hundred other reasons besides truth: relevance, practicality, advantage, comfort, interest, dynamism, challenge, power, novelty, happiness."

In other words, it's not enough to simply believe, yes, God is relevant. Is there any ascertainable truth to the possibility that we can know God and experience a vital relationship with him?

While granting that theologians don't have a corner on wisdom or knowledge, Carl F. H. Henry says that "truth is Christianity's supreme asset." Humbly, we must acknowledge that God alone surely knows all. Such humility "becomes scientists as well as theologians," Henry says.

Christianity does claim, however, that God has indeed revealed a vast body of truth to humanity with the purpose of helping us come into a vital relationship with him. Scripture doesn't answer every minute wondering of the inquiring mind, but it does address all the central, urgent issues. And it gives wisdom for making right decisions.

Christian writer William H. Willimon puts it well: "The Bible does not address all contemporary human questions, but perhaps the Bible wants to rearrange our questions, to entice us away from our merely contemporary infatuations, to take us places we would not have gone without the prodding of the Bible."

Scripture addresses not only many of our felt needs but also our real needs as God diagnoses them.

HOW DO WE KNOW?

What I'm affirming, then, is that it *is* possible to determine good accurate answers to big questions, in areas of science, theology, history, and other branches of learning. And it's equally possible to determine that certain other answers are simply wrong.

From where do we derive good answers? From a variety of sources, including:

- what we learn propositionally, from the Bible. This is the supreme source of truth for Christians.
- what we know historically
- what we reason intellectually
- what we discover experientially
- what we discern relationally
- what we feel intuitively
- what we test scientifically

By drawing on all these sources of truth, in the spirit of Blaise Pascal (Chapter 8), we may test the truth value of proposed answers to life's questions.

Yet does what we learn propositionally from the Scriptures always agree with other sources of truth? Let's consider one example:

When asked by an expert in Mosaic law to name the greatest of its six hundred thirteen commandments, Jesus Christ answered: " 'Love the Lord your God with all your heart and with all your soul and with all your mind.' This is the first and greatest commandment. And the second is like it: 'Love your neighbor as yourself.' All of Law and Prophets hang on these two commandments" (Matthew 22:37–40).

Historically, how truthful is Jesus' answer? Reviewing the ancient Jewish Scriptures, we know Jesus accurately quoted two key verses penned by Moses. Judging from the response that Jesus received to his answer, and comparing the writings of other Jewish rabbis, it's clear that Jesus also gave a good answer.

Intellectually, how truthful is Jesus' answer? Logically, from a monotheistic point of view, it makes sense. It gives priority to our vertical relationship with God and our horizontal relationships with others, while affirming self-worth.

Experientially, relationally, and *intuitively,* how truthful is Jesus' answer? Millions of Christians claim they find much wisdom in his words. As late as 1930, however, Freud scorned them. Within three years, however, in an open letter to Einstein, Freud spoke of love "without a sexual aim" as the only way to stand against the unspeakable evil of another world war. In that letter, Freud noted: "There is no need for psycho-analysis to be ashamed to speak of love in this connection, for religion itself uses the same words: 'Thou shalt love thy neighbor as thyself.' " Freud had come around to see the timeless truth of God's inspired word.

Scientifically, how truthful is Jesus' answer? That's impossible to say, since the issue at hand is nonphysical: like most of life, it's outside the realm of scientific inquiry.

That most important truth statements cannot be proved scientifically shouldn't disturb us. Science is but one test of truthfulness, applicable to only certain limited areas of knowledge or potential knowledge.

The Scriptures, other propositional writings, histories, experiences, relationships, intuitive feelings all contribute to our knowledge and understanding of life.

Overall, how reliable are the Scriptures? Are they indeed the revealed, inspired, infallible Word of God, as the Christian Church has taught and believed?

CAN WE TAKE GOD AT HIS WORD?

When American radio's leading bad boy pitched his shock-jock book on "The Tonight Show with Jay Leno," Howard Stern claimed it was "the fastest-selling book in the history of books." To make his point, Stern held up a Bible and announced, "The Gideon Company is now putting *my* book in the place of Bibles in hotels." In a moment of courage, an incensed Leno took the Bible out of his guest's hand and publicly rebuked Stern for blaspheming God's word.

The fact is, the Bible so far outsells every other book year after year that it's never named on the *New York Times* best-seller list. It's a given. According to the Chicago Tribune News Service, Bibles sold through retail outlets generate more than $500 million in sales annually. No other book, especially Stern's bawdy work, ever comes a close second.

When asked in a recent national poll, "What book would you say has been the most influential in the course of human history?" eighty percent of American adults said the Bible. Other titles weren't even close. A very distant second and third? Benjamin Spock's *Common Sense Book of Baby and Child Care* and Charles Darwin's *Origin of Species,* with five and four percent of the votes, respectively.

Opinion polls are just that—people's opinions. Many thinkers would agree that the works of Nietzsche, Marx, and other writers have had much more influence (horrific, of course) on the course of history in recent generations than Spock's volume.

Still, at the dawn of the third millennium after the time of Jesus Christ, it's remarkable that most Americans embrace a book compiled nearly two millennia ago from the writings of approximately forty writers, some of whom were penning their chapters fourteen hundred years before Christ.

A full three out of four adults (seventy-six percent) say Bible reading is important to them, and one in six (seventeen percent) read it daily. Even among baby busters (eighteen- to thirty-year-olds), more than eighty percent say they own and want to read the entire Bible.

Why such interest in reading an old book? I believe because it is God's Word, filled with compelling narratives found from cover to cover.

David Suchet, of Hercule Poirot fame on PBS's *Mystery!* program, also plays Aaron in *Moses,* TNT's fourth Old Testament epic. In an interview, Suchet said he welcomed the opportunity to play Moses' brother and explore the Bible.

"These wonderful stories that are found in the Old Testament and the New, they're glorious," says Suchet. "I don't find them dusty; I find them full of humanity, full of reality, full of drama."

The TNT epic touched on Suchet's personal interests: around family and job commitments, he is working on a degree in theology.

"I think it's one of the most fundamental, important issues of our day," he says. "I'm quite religious anyway. But irrespective of that, I'm appalled at what mankind has done to religion."

What we've done to religion is most appalling indeed. We've either pitied religion to death, reinvented it in our own (marred) image, devolved it into something pagan, wielded it for political power, sold it out for commercial gain, or—worst of all—transformed it into the worship of self.

The Bible tells a host of wonderful historical case studies about real people, real problems, and—I emphatically believe—real encounters with God.

As literature, the Bible's influence is unparalleled. One of the founders of America's leading news magazine, Henry Luce, once admitted: "*Time* did not invent personality journalism. The Bible did." The Old and New Testaments, however, don't just tell good stories. The theme of God's relevance fills the pages of this divine revelation.

According to *Time,* "the Bible underlies so much of Western culture that it matters a great deal whether its narratives are grounded in truth."

So what's the verdict? *Time* says: "Few scholars believe that miracles like Moses' burning bush or Jesus' resurrection will ever be proved scientifically; they are, after all, supernatural events. Conversely, few doubt that the characters in the latter part of the Old Testament and most of the New—Nebuchadnezzar, Jeremiah, Jesus, Peter—really existed, though some will always doubt parts of their stories."

With a bit of hyperbole, *Time* continues: "The historical accuracy of much of the Bible could be settled, one way or the other, almost at a stroke."

So how relevant is the Bible? In a university commencement address, Ted Koppel stated: "Our society finds Truth too strong a medicine to digest undiluted. In its purest form Truth is not a polite tap on the shoulder; it is a howling reproach. What Moses brought down from Mount Sinai were not the Ten Suggestions . . . they are commandments. Are, not were."

The truth of God is more than commandments, of course. The apostle Peter himself says that God has given us "very great and precious promises" (2 Peter 1:4).

What are some of those promises?

First, *God loves us and wants us to enter into a vital relationship with him.* What could be more incredible than that the God of the universe knows and loves us? Yet this is what Scripture promises.

St. John wrote, "For God so loved the world that he gave his one and only Son, that whoever believes in him shall not perish but have eternal life" (John 3:16).

Jesus himself told his disciples: " 'I have loved you. Greater love has no one than this, that he lay down his life for his friends. You are my friends' " (John 15:12–14).

The apostle Paul wrote, "For I am convinced that neither death nor life, neither angels nor demons, neither the present nor the future, nor any powers, neither height nor depth, nor anything else in all creation, will be able to separate us from the love of God that is in Christ Jesus our Lord" (Romans 8:38–39).

Have you experienced that love yet?

Second, *God longs to give us a new heart and forgive our sins.* The bad news is that we all have a fatal heart disease: sin. Our souls are bent toward evil. The good news is that God has made a remarkable, costly provision to forgive our sins.

The prophet Jeremiah wrote that a time was coming when God would make a new covenant with his people, written on their hearts: " 'they will all know me, from the least of them to the greatest,' declares the LORD. 'For I will forgive their wickedness and will remember their sins no more' " (Jeremiah 31:24).

Paul wrote: "God has poured out his love into our hearts by the Holy Spirit, whom he has given us. You see, at just the right time, Christ died for the ungodly. Very rarely will anyone die for a righteous man, though for a good man someone might possibly dare to die. But God demonstrated his own love for us in this: While we were still sinners, Christ died for us" (Romans 5:6–8).

Have you experienced that forgiveness yet?

Third, *God invites us to become part of his family forever.* We can become sons and daughters of the King of kings.

The prophet Hosea spoke of a time of repentance, forgiveness, and restoration: "In the place where it was said to them, 'You are not my people,' they will be called 'sons of the living God' " (Hosea 1:10).

John wrote that many rejected Jesus Christ when he came to earth: "Yet to all who received him, to those who believed in his name, he gave the right to become children of God" (John 1:12).

Peter adds that those who believe have become "a chosen people, a royal priesthood, a holy nation, a people belonging to God, that you may declare the praises of him who called you out of darkness into his wonderful light. Once you were not a people, but now you are the people of God" (1 Peter 2:9–10).

Have you become a new person in Jesus Christ yet? God's promises are yours for the taking.

IS THE BIBLE RELIABLE?

What evidence do we have to suggest that God's promises recorded in the Bible are trustworthy? Like any other ancient documents, the reliability of the Scriptures can be ascertained by:

- the historical verifiability of the manuscript
- the number of manuscripts
- the age of the manuscripts
- the accuracy of the manuscripts
- other manuscript evidence

In the last century, the entire Bible has been subjected to intense scrutiny by historians and archeologists—far more than any other book. The verdict? Allow me to focus on the New Testament findings for a minute.

On all accounts, scholars have concluded that the New Testament canon is far more reliable than all other ancient Greek and Latin texts put together. Why? The sacredness of these writings compelled the early Christians to make numerous copies soon after the originals were written. Those copies were made with meticulous care and often were quoted in their other writings.

The historicity of the New Testament is extremely well documented. What we know of Aristotle, Plato, and Socrates rests on much less solid ground. When Dr. John Warwick Montgomery debated philosophy professor Avrum Stroll of the University of British Columbia, Stroll had to concede this point. Yet rather than accept the New Testament at face value, for what it says, Stroll decided instead to "throw out my knowledge of the classical world."

To which the chairman of the classics department exclaimed: "Good Lord, Avrum, not *that!*"

The question isn't, Are the New Testament documents reliable? But, Are they trustworthy?

Consider the options.

Option No. 1. The writers were disciples of Jesus Christ who recorded accurately what they saw and heard. What they saw and heard was unique (and so powerful) that it captivated them and changed their lives. Within a generation after Jesus Christ stepped off the scene, they recorded what they had seen and heard so others would be captivated by the same message—and person—and have their lives changed, too.

Option No. 2. Or the writers were followers of Jesus Christ who in their zeal "divinized" him after his death. Their intentions were supposedly good, but their writings and teaching don't correspond with reality. Instead, their writings represent idealistic Messianic wish fulfillment, nothing more.

Option No. 3. Or the writers maliciously "divinized" Jesus for their own selfish ends. They hoped to profit by the creation of a new, "superior" religion to replace Judaism, which was under attack and, for all practical purposes, soon to be destroyed.

The last option is ludicrous: all the evidence points in the other direction. It was Christianity, not Judaism, that came under the fiercest of attacks. As Pascal pointed out, why would the writers subject themselves to intense persecution and brutal martyrdom to perpetrate what they knew full well was a blatant hoax?

The second option is equally preposterous: too many other people knew Jesus. Tens of thousands had listened to what he said, had seen what he did, and knew that he'd died. How could they have possibly thought they could get away with the idea that Jesus was indeed God's Son, raised from the dead, unless the truth was on their side?

The first option is the only rational explanation. All other options pale in comparison. The writings of the New Testament—miracles, prophecies, and all—have the ring of truth as C. S. Lewis used to say. He turned from atheism to classic Christianity after noting, among other things, that mythmakers and false religionists don't write like this.

Yet what about all the *miracles?* Are they believable?

Following philosopher David Hume, many dismiss biblical miracles out of hand, even when they know better. John H. Gerstner noted: "One of the most outstanding Biblical scholars in the country once said publicly, in answer to a question concerning his interpretation of miracles in the Old Testament, 'When I meet an alleged miracle, I simply treat it as legend.'" In other words, Gerstner says, "He knows in advance that any and all alleged miracles are legends merely. But how does he know it? He does not know it; he merely declares it."

That most of life follows natural law doesn't disprove the supernatural, or vice versa. "When one argues for the occasional miracle," Gerstner said, "he is in the same breath arguing for the usually nonmiraculous."

Gerstner rejects the idea, promoted by some, that quantum theory and indeterminism ("unpredictable behavior in the laws of nature") provide a modern explanation of biblical miracles. Why? Miracles are supernatural; indeterminism simply allows for the theoretical possibility that natural law doesn't always hold.

And what about all the *prophecies?*

If God can intervene in human history (miracles), it follows that he also can predict human history (prophecy). And predict he does: hundreds upon hundreds of specific predictions about the Jewish people and their promised Messiah.

When Frederick the Great demanded, "Give me, in one word, a proof of the truth of the Bible," he was told by his chaplain, "The Jews." Just as easily, he might have been told, "The Christ."

As a skeptic, Hugh Ross (with the help of several equally skeptical friends) calculated the probability "of the chance fulfillment of thirteen Bible predictions about specific people and their specific actions. My conservative estimate showed less than one chance in 10^{138} that such predictions could come true without supernatural intervention." Since earning his Ph.D. in astronomy at the University of Toronto, Ross has become an articulate spokesman *for* classic Christian belief.

Peter Stoner, former chair of the department of mathematics and astronomy at Pasadena City College and later chair of the department of science at Westmont, analyzed forty-eight specific Jewish predictions about the coming Messiah, all written more than two hundred fifty years before Jesus Christ's birth, and concluded: "We find the chance that any one man fulfilled all forty-eight prophecies to be 1 in 10^{157}." The biblical writers could not have achieved such unbelievable accuracy—unless God revealed to them what to write.

The odds against fallible men predicting the future on their own, without God, stagger the imagination. Picture the entire state of Texas covered in silver dollars two feet deep. One of those silver dollars is specially marked. Blindfold someone and ask him to walk across the state for a few weeks and then randomly select that one silver dollar. What are the chances of success? Only 1 in 10^{17}.

Picture the rest of the contiguous United States covered in silver dollars two feet deep. Again, blindfold someone and ask him to walk across the nation for a few months and then randomly select one specially marked silver dollar, first try. That's 1 in 10^{18}.

Picture the vast continents of Africa and Asia covered in silver dollars two feet deep. Ask someone to walk for a few years and then randomly select one specially marked coin. That's 1 in 10^{19}.

The point is: in a hundred billion years, there's no chance the biblical prophecies about Jesus Christ ever would have been fulfilled—unless God deliberately chose to step into human history.

In popular appeal, in historical detail, in literary quality, in manuscript reliability, and in predictive accuracy, the biblical Scriptures have no equal whatsoever—they far surpass all other literature.

Feuerbach, Freud, and their soul mates were more than a bit rash in citing "science" as an excuse to unceremoniously curse God, shred the Bible, and then encourage their followers to do the same.

Their pride and arrogance are actually rather shocking, especially given the tragic results of their militant atheism this past century.

A SCIENTIST'S STORY

After a luncheon in one of America's largest cities, an elderly man slowly walked toward me, each step a struggle on impaired legs. He introduced himself. I was talking to a retired university professor, age seventy-seven, who once was a candidate for the Nobel prize in chemistry. I asked him, "Do you have eternal life, or are you still searching?"

He answered, "My wife's going to heaven, and I'm going to hell."

"That's interesting," I thought. "I didn't ask him that."

"Professor, why do you say that you're going to hell?"

"When I was a boy, I had faith, and then I lost it," he said. "Now it's too late."

"Professor, it's never too late. Besides, you came to talk to me because you want to know, don't you?"

"Yes," he said, "I do."

"When did you lose your faith?"

"In college. They took it from me at the university, and I've been forty years without faith. God will never take me back."

"Yes, he will take you back."

"No, he won't. . . . He can't."

"Professor, why do you say that?"

"Because I am so unworthy, that's why. I'm so unworthy."

"Professor, you're right. You are unworthy. But so am I, and so is the rest of the human race."

It was Holy Week, so I said, "Why do you think we celebrate Good Friday? The cross, Professor. On the cross is where God took care of our guilt and our sin, and he buried it forever. Professor, you really want to be forgiven, don't you?"

"Yes, I do."

"Professor, God can take away your guilt—even forty years' worth. Listen to what he says in the Bible: 'Their sins and evil deeds I will remember no more' " (Hebrews 10:17).

"That's beautiful," he said.

"Are you ready to be received back by God?"

"I am."

I put my arm around this distinguished elderly gentleman and prayed with him. He was trembling as he opened his heart to Jesus Christ.

About two weeks later, at a luncheon for women, I told this distinguished scientist's story. Afterward, up came an elderly woman. "I'm the professor's wife," she said.

"Did I tell the story right?"

"I don't know, I wasn't there," she said. "But I'll tell you something. My husband is more certain than I am that I'm going to heaven. I'm not certain at all."

"Why do you say you're not certain?" I asked.

"Because I've let God down so many times. I've gone to church all my life, but I feel I never quite measure up."

"Madam, if not letting God down is a condition for going to heaven, we've all had it, because we've all let him down. Heaven is a gift, a gift of the mercy of God."

She understood, and from that moment her hope in heaven moved from good works to God's work on the cross.

A few weeks later I spoke to this couple on the phone. "Thank you," they said, for pointing the way to eternal life through Jesus Christ. "We are now both sure that we have eternal life."

I find most people feel unworthy of forgiveness. They have a tremendous sense of unworthiness, even if outwardly they are antagonistic toward God and the gospel. If you peel off the layers, the antagonist would say: "If there is a God, I'm going to hell. God would never forgive me."

When *Time* magazine asked in a poll whether Americans today believe in miracles, sixty-nine percent said yes. Why is it, then, that we're so reluctant to believe in the miracle of God's forgiveness of sins?

Church historian Martin Marty says: "Miracles can occur without special effects. It takes more doing for a holy God to forgive an errant person than it does to part the waters of the sea."

Yet that's God's specialty.

Part II

FACING THE FUTURE

CHAPTER 5

CHANGE FOR THE BETTER?

How much does it matter whether or not you and I embrace belief in God?

During a Christian rally some years ago, a heckler shouted, "Atheism has done more for the world than Christianity!"

"Very well," the speaker said, "tomorrow night you bring a hundred men whose lives have been changed for the better by atheism, and I'll bring a hundred who have been transformed by Christ."

The heckler frowned and said no more.

Why?

I think the facts speak for themselves.

René Girard once suggested, "Since the attempt to understand religion on the basis of philosophy has failed, we ought to try the reverse method and read philosophy in the light of religion." The results prove interesting.

Christian theologian J. I. Packer and Thomas Howard summarize the philosophies of the apostles of atheism this way:

- Ludwig Feuerbach: "Religion means childlike immaturity."
- Karl Marx: "Atheism is a necessity, since all religions support unjust social structures."
- Friedrich Nietzsche: "Now that God is dead, everything is permissible."
- Sigmund Freud: "Religion is an illusion, a wish-fulfillment fantasy."

Based on the light of true religion, however, the fact is:

- in contrast to Feuerbach: "Childlike faith in God is the foundation for true maturity."
- in contrast to Marx: "Belief in God is a necessity, since all atheistic systems, most notably Marxism, support unjust social structures."
- in contrast to Nietzsche: "Because God is alive, all things are possible."
- in contrast to Freud: "Atheism is an illusion, a wish-fulfillment fantasy."

In his massive, thoroughly documented 800-page analysis of atheistic philosophical thought over the past four centuries, renowned German theologian Hans Küng claims it is more reasonable and perhaps easier "today than a few decades or even centuries ago" to believe in God. Why? Because after watching atheism proliferate over the past century, and witnessing the tragic results, it's clearer than ever that God is relevant to the well-being and future of individuals, couples, families, communities, and even nations.

Without God, we're lost.

NO MORE HIDE-AND-SEEK

In moments of intellectual honesty, even some of the most committed atheists agree that life makes sense only if God is in the picture.

At the beginning of this book, I told the story of Jean-Paul Sartre's change of heart. Shortly before his death, Sartre could no longer read or write. Yet he continued to propagate his latest ideas in a series of interviews.

During one of those interviews, Sartre told a Marxist journalist that he had come to belief in God. His words are worth repeating: "I do not feel that I am the product of chance, a speck of dust in the universe, but someone who was expected, prepared, prefigured. In short, a being whom only a Creator could put here; and this idea of a creating hand refers to God."

Not unlike many in his generation, author David Manning White admitted: "For most of my life I permitted myself a grudging half-search for God without really wanting to come to grips with the awe-striking magnitude of his presence at the absolute core of my existence. The intense, egotistic clamor with which I sought to understand the world and its travails virtually precluded anything more than a de facto acknowledgment that I might possess a spiritual self."

Katharine Tait had this to say about her famous father, Bertrand Russell: "Somewhere at the back of my father's mind, at the bottom of his heart, in the depths of his soul, there was an empty space that had once been filled by God and he never found anything else to put in it." Russell himself once admitted: "The center of me is always and eternally a terrible pain—a curious wild pain—a searching for something beyond what the world contains."

Echoing what I've heard from many other young adults, "Generation X" author Douglas Copeland says, in almost hushed tones: "Now—here's my secret: I tell it to you with an openness of heart that I doubt I shall ever achieve again, so I pray that you are in a quiet room as you hear these words. My secret is that I need God—that I am sick and can no longer make it alone. I need God to help me give, because I no longer seem capable of giving; to help me be kind, because I no longer seem capable of kindness; to help me love, as I seem beyond being able to love."

Today, after a long battle, we're finally willing again to confess that we need God. We always have. After St. Augustine converted to Christianity, the great fifth-century philosopher wrote this confession: "You have made us for Yourself and our hearts are restless until they find their rest in You."

Later, Pascal echoed his words, writing: "There is a God-shaped vacuum in the heart of every man, and only God can fill it."

In one of his best-selling books, Harold Kushner says there's still a "spiritual vacuum at the center" of the lives of people today. Why? He contends many are looking for purpose, fulfillment, and meaning in their work or in their families, only later coming to the realization that doesn't work.

Kushner claims "there is a kind of nourishment our souls crave, even as our bodies need the right foods, sunshine, and exercise. Without that spiritual nourishment, our souls remain stunted and undeveloped."

FINDING THE GOD WHO IS

The key, however, isn't tapping into spirituality for our own benefit. Christian author Patrick M. Morley is right: "There's a God we want and there's a God who is and they are not the same God. The turning point comes when we stop seeking the God we want and start seeking the God who is."

R. C. Sproul suggests that, even if we feel attracted to the idea of "God," the thought of encountering God as he truly is can be frightening. While someone "may desire and create for himself a deity who meets his needs and provides him with innumerable benefits," Sproul says, "he will not [naturally] desire a God who is holy, omniscient, and sovereign."

Peter Kreeft agrees: "I'm convinced that many people reject Christianity—traditional, biblical, orthodox Christianity, with its active, loving, interfering, demanding God—for that reason. Not because the evidence proves it's untrue, but because they don't *want* it to be true."

A successful businessman once told me, "I'm afraid of meeting God," of getting to know him personally. God seemed too awesome to approach.

Yet experiencing the holiness, omniscience, and sovereignty of the active, loving, interfering, demanding God of heaven and earth is precisely what we need:

"Repent, then, and turn to God, so that your sins may be wiped out, that times of refreshing may come from the Lord, and that he may send the Christ, who has been appointed for you—even Jesus. He must remain in heaven until the time comes for God to restore everything, as he promised long ago through his holy prophets" (Acts 3:19–21).

"But when the kindness and love of God our Savior appeared, he saved us, not because of righteous things we had done, but because of his mercy. He saved us through the washing of rebirth and renewal by the Holy Spirit, whom he poured out on us generously through Jesus Christ our Savior" (Titus 3:4–6).

"Taste and see that the Lord is good; blessed is the man who takes refuge in him" (Psalm 34:8).

G. K. Chesterton was right: "The problem with Christianity is not that it has been tried and found wanting, but that it has been found difficult, and left untried."

A few months ago the New York Mills Cultural Center sponsored the fourth annual Great American Think-off. Thanks to publicity in *U.S. News & World Report, USA Today,* and National Public Radio, the philosophical contest drew nearly seven hundred entrants from forty states. Doctors, executives, farmers, homemakers, musicians, truck drivers, waitresses, and others from various walks of life submitted essays on the question "Does God exist? If yes, why; if no, why not?"

The contest's only content requirement was that entrants draw on personal experience alone. That certainly made for a more colorful competition. Jeremy Jacobs, member of the alternative rock band Mr. Neutron, led a contingent of forty-three entrants who claimed that God doesn't exist. Jacobs's personal reason: he thought, at age twenty-five, that he could do a better job of running the universe.

The contest's winner, Charles Eginton, a retired surgeon, cited "several supernatural phenomena which occurred during the course of my professional career," plus the experiences of every other surgeon he knew, demonstrating "the presence of God in their work" as "overwhelming circumstantial evidence that God does, indeed, exist." An M.D. friend of mine puts it this way: "I do the surgery, God does the healing."

Based on personal experience alone, the sheer fact that hundreds of millions of people around the world believe in God is compelling.

Edith Stein, German philosopher Edmund Husserl's famous assistant, discarded her atheistic beliefs at once after witnessing Jesus Christ's presence in a new widow's life. Later, she wrote: "In this, my first encounter with the cross and with the divine force which it communicates to the person who carries it, I saw, for the first time and tangibly before me, the Church born of the redeeming suffering of Christ in His victory over the sting of death. This was the moment when my disbelief collapsed and Christ rose resplendent before me, the Christ in the mystery of the cross."

New York Herald reporter Henry Stanley converted to Jesus Christ after a lengthy expedition into the wilds of Africa to find the legendary Dr. David Livingstone. Most people have heard the famous story about Stanley finding Dr. Livingstone after several months of intense searching. What many haven't heard is that Stanley was deeply moved by this Christian missionary-explorer's inner peace and strength, and ended up trusting Jesus Christ as Savior.

Later Stanley wrote: "I went to Africa as prejudiced against religion as the worst infidel in London. . . . For months after we met I found myself listening to him [Livingstone], wondering at the old man carrying out the words [of Jesus Christ], 'leave all and follow me.' But little by little, seeing his piety, his gentleness, his zeal, his earnestness, and how he went quietly about his business, I was converted by him, although he had not tried to do it."

In the capital city of one country, I had a packed speaking tour. As if a full schedule every day wasn't enough, I had to race from the stadium to the television studios of Channel 4 every night for a live one-hour program, taking calls from viewers all across the nation.

Back at the hotel one night, I had just gone to my room when the phone rang. The desk clerk said someone in the bar by the lobby was anxious to talk with me. It was 1:45 A.M. My first thought was, "I've been up since seven yesterday morning, and now some drunk wants to talk!"

I went to the lobby to find a rather distinguished-looking gentleman waiting for me. He was visibly shaking. "I watched your program three hours ago," he said, "and it hit home to my problem. I began to weep and my teenage daughter said, 'Dad, why don't you go and talk to him? He might be able to help you with your drinking problem.' "

Not only did he have a drinking problem, he also confessed he was persistently unfaithful to his wife, even though he was a well-known psychologist who counseled others. "I can't control myself. I'm living like a dog!" He pounded his fist on the coffee table, then pleaded: "Is there any hope of change for a hypocrite like me?"

Several people had strolled out of the hotel bar and were in the lobby watching from a distance. I presented the good news of Jesus Christ and his almighty power to my less than sober psychologist friend. I've seldom dealt with such an earnest man. Finally he said, "I want to receive Christ right now." He got on his knees in the middle of the lobby, where I led him in a prayer of salvation.

A week later, during our final live television broadcast, the very last phone call went like this: "Mr. Palau, do you remember the man you talked to until three in the morning in the hotel? That's me."

I had to ask, "Have you experienced any change this past week?"

"A complete change! And now my wife wants to talk to you." This conversation was going out nationwide.

"Have you seen a change in your husband this past week?" I asked. Not only had she, but she wanted to invite Jesus Christ into her life, too.

Such experiences aren't the only compelling reason for you and me to enter into a vital relationship with God. If I had never heard of anyone who believed in God, I would still believe that God is worthy of my wholehearted devotion, worship, obedience, and love simply from reading the Scriptures, to say nothing of other compelling arguments in God's favor.

More than ten years ago, *Time* magazine reported: "In a quiet revolution in thought and argument that hardly anyone would have foreseen only two decades ago, God is making a comeback. Most intriguingly this is happening . . . in the crisp intellectual circles of academic philosophers."

Mortimer Adler, one of America's most influential philosophers of the past half century, surveyed all the great writings for and against God, analyzed their arguments, and then wrote an essay affirming: "I am persuaded that God exists, either beyond a reasonable doubt or by a preponderance of reasons in favor of that conclusion over reasons against it."

Kreeft says: "The idea of God has guided or deluded more lives, changed more history, inspired more music and poetry and philosophy than anything else, real or imagined. . . . [S]uppose no one in history had ever conceived the idea of God. Now, rewrite history following that premise." It doesn't work.

CAN SO MANY BE SO WRONG?

Hans Küng finds Feuerbach's dire predictions of the imminent disappearance of Christianity almost comic to read today, if it weren't for the truly horrific results of his thoroughgoing antitheism. Almost twenty years ago, Küng already was asking: "Even without Auschwitz and the Gulag Archipelago, in East and West, has not atheism lost credibility: in both nature science and medicine, in both politics and culture?"

Atheism has lost most of its credibility as we enter the twenty-first century. Not that it might not make a comeback. Mark Twain once remarked, "One of the most striking differences between a cat and a lie is that a cat has only nine lives." If the current interest in spirituality ends up becoming nothing more than a rather bizarre fad, atheism may roar back to life with even more devastating results sometime within the next generation and a half.

A Yiddish proverb says, "A half truth is a whole lie." Misguided spirituality is half right: we need God in our lives. Pick-and-choose religion is not the answer; logically, how could it be?

The sad fact is, to be illogical is all too human. Professor Irving M. Copi observed: "It is interesting that in logic courses at the university level dealing with such formal questions and dealing with examples of fallacies, students are often presented with passages taken not from the lower classes of literature, such as comic books or tabloids or propaganda manuscripts, but from the finest literary products of western culture. Passages from John Stuart Mill, David Hume, Immanuel Kant, Aristotle, Cicero, etc., are used as illustrations of examples of blatant logical fallacies present in the works of the most learned men."

If the greatest thinkers get it wrong, what hope is there for you and me? This: if we're paying attention, we don't have to repeat the terrible errors of the past (outlined in more detail in Part III).

The irrationality of the late twentieth century bears tragic witness to the intellectual bankruptcy of the apostles of atheism. Their now aging appeals to "science" have sent millions off the deep end into despair à la Sartre and Russell, into psychedelic experiences à la Aldous Huxley and Timothy Leary, and into mysticism and occultism à la Shirley MacLaine and others.

Oblivious to the potentially fatal consequences of their actions, Feuerbach, Marx, Nietzsche, and Freud used nonrational, magical thinking to convince themselves—and others—that, if they thought God and the Bible were irrelevant, it was so.

Scott Peck observes: "Magical thinking can take a variety of forms, but basically it is a belief that thoughts in and of themselves may cause events to occur." Children think like this; adults should know better.

Like Don Quixote, the apostles of atheism were "tilting at windmills." That is, they were taking on a supposedly "noble" but utterly idealistic/unrealistic/impractical/impossible task, owing to delusional notions of who they were, what reality is, and how they might change the future.

Sir Harold Bowden warned, "Facts that are not frankly faced have a habit of stabbing us in the back."

The apostles of atheism were adamantly unwilling to consider the facts about God and the Bible, and instead (for personal reasons) opposed them with all their might.

Sproul reminds us that "the matter of the knowledge of God the Creator is not so much an intellectual problem as it is a moral problem." Why would anyone not frankly face the truth? Sproul suggests, "simply because the lie seems easier to live with."

We are the children of such lies.

Time essayist Charles Krauthammer bemoans America's "flight toward irrationality," our "retreat to prescientific primitivism in an age that otherwise preens with scientific pride." Especially beguiling, he says, "is that irrationalism is gaining official sanction."

Krauthammer goes on to say: "And what should we expect in an age in which John Mack, a Harvard professor of psychiatry, publishes a book on the abduction of humans by aliens—he is particularly fascinated with the way aliens inseminate our womenfolk—and . . . What? Is fired? Denied tenure? Hardly. Finds himself with a best seller, a spot on *Oprah* and a fistful of Rockefeller-family research money."

He adds, "Why these outbreaks of irrationalism? Because in a highly technological age . . . the need for escape is powerful." So, for intellectual relaxation, "we give rapt attention to bearers of tales."

Like Krauthammer, I cringe at the nonsense some people believe. Yet I have to wonder: historically, what age hasn't believed tall tales? For all our scientific advances, human nature hasn't changed. We've always been ready for another far-fetched, titillating saga.

Granted, something is seriously skewed when a person entertains and embraces irrationality. The antidote to irrationalism, however, isn't pure rationalism. After all, we humans are rather complex creatures. Each person possesses incredible intellectual, emotional, volitional, social, and spiritual capacities for good or evil. We're not *mind,* alone.

GETTING IT RIGHT, TOGETHER

Biblical Christianity calls us to love God with all our heart, and soul, and strength, *and* mind. In that, it is the sanest belief system of all—it addresses you and me, as persons, in our totality. Together, not in isolation.

Ultimately, belief in God is something I do in community. Why? Because in the community of a solid Christian church I experience God in the context of relationships. Because there I also learn "the whole counsel of God," saving me from undue errors.

What I present in this book as classic Christianity, then, doesn't originate with me. The essential message certainly isn't unique. The New Testament demonstrates that the apostle Paul and the other apostles of Jesus preached the same message nearly two millennia ago. Even atheist Bernard Williams admits, "Christianity is a religion which is very historically articulate." What has been believed from the time of Jesus Christ until today is verifiable: any good book on world history can confirm what I'm saying.

Still, I recognize my inherent vulnerability to giving the classic Christian message my own twist, thus corrupting it. That's why I asked several well-respected theologians (among many others listed in the acknowledgments) to review drafts of this book. The final result and any faults are mine alone, of course. But my greatest desire is to effectively communicate to you (and other readers) that belief in God makes sense—for all of life.

Like the apostle Paul, who advocated "reasonable spiritual worship," I see no need to appeal to irrationalism to make my case. Classic Christianity is the most rational, emotionally satisfying, volitionally motivating, socially uplifting, and spiritually regenerating religion in the world.

As you continue reading, ask yourself: "Do I want to enter into relationship with God?" and "If I do, what difference will it make?"

PHILIP'S STORY

What difference can God make in your life? Just ask Philip, an international soccer star from Australia:

"I grew up in a Christian home and went to church mainly for friendship and activity, but I had no real interest in the Christian faith. I knew, if I did, I would have to give up going to bars and chasing women, and probably give up soccer as well.

"I was young, keen, super fit, with the sporting world at my feet. But I began to wonder, 'Where am I going? What's the point? There must be more to life than this.'

"I knew Christ was there but he had to have me totally. I didn't want any inhibitions. I didn't want anyone telling me what to do and so I decided to leave Australia and go overseas, traveling with a group keen on drinking, partying, bed swapping, and the like as we traveled around Western Europe.

"Even then, I felt as if I had no real friends. There was a sense of loneliness roaming around like that. Life was pointless and meaningless. I knew there had to be something more.

"I decided to settle down for a while in England and, at the encouragement of my parents and Christian friends back home, linked up with a church nearby. They immediately made me feel as if I belonged.

"With a group from that fellowship, I went to a large soccer stadium to hear Luis Palau. That evening Luis challenged his audience to stop playing games and get serious about Jesus Christ. From the Bible, he showed that God had sent his Son so that all may know him through the power of the life, death, and resurrection of Jesus Christ.

"That night, this prodigal son's life was turned around. I'm so glad to be finally 'back home,' part of God's forever family."

Chapter 6

WHO IS JESUS?

The message of classic Christianity is centered in a person. You can have Confucianism without Confucius, Buddhism without Buddha, and Judaism without Abraham or Moses.

Christianity is different. Relationship with Jesus Christ is the origin, motivation, and goal of the classic Christian faith. This requires belief that Jesus Christ is alive, that he is divine, and that he is still inviting us to know him personally.

In the Bible, Jesus says: "I am standing at the door of your heart and knocking. If anyone hears my voice and opens the door, I will come in and eat with him, and he with me" (Revelation 3:20).

IS HE DIVINE?

Confucius never claimed he could knock on the door of someone's heart.

Buddha rejected India's multiplicity of gods and never claimed to be one himself.

Abraham and Moses certainly never taught that they were God incarnate.

Of all the great sages and prophets throughout world history, Jesus alone claimed to be God-become-man.

Peter Kreeft says that Jesus Christ's claim of divinity is "the most extreme claim anyone ever made."

The Jehovah's Witnesses, the infamous Jesus Seminar, and other groups have actively sought to deny Jesus' divinity. But following the example of David Friedrich Strauss, you first have to throw out three hundred pages of historical data.

What do those data reveal about Jesus' identity?

Time, Life, Newsweek, U.S. News & World Report, and other national news magazines have examined this question with numerous cover stories during the past three years. A host of talk shows and programs, including A&E's much-hyped *Jesus: A Biography,* have been asking the same thing. Some have taken offense that the media would ask such a potentially threatening question, but I applaud their efforts. Asking questions doesn't mean I'm a skeptic. Even Jesus asked his disciples, "Who do you say I am?"

Well, who is he?

According to the Jesus Seminar panelists, Jesus was a poor Jewish carpenter turned cynical sage who healed people's hurts, used liberal doses of irony and humor to salt his teachings, came into conflict with the prevailing religious powers, caught the wrath of the Roman governor, and died like a common criminal. End of story.

After years searching for "the historical Jesus," Robert Funk of the Jesus Seminar claims to have proved that starting a new religion "would have been the farthest thing from [Jesus'] mind." To deconstruct Christianity, then, Funk has set out to create what he calls "a new fiction, a new narrative, a new gospel."

In a letter to *Time* about the Jesus Seminar, Eleanor McKee put it well: "Let's see if I got it straight. Fifty panelists, one of whom directed *Showgirls,* have determined that 1.5 billion misguided Christians have an erroneous impression of who Jesus was. A more accurate version of the life of Christ was created by a vote that involved dropping plastic beads into a bucket. O ye of little faith!"

Peter Kreeft contends that such critics use circular arguments to dismiss the divine claims and miracles of Jesus. They dismiss them because the biblical text is supposedly in doubt, *and then* turn around and dismiss the text because the divine claims and miracles of Jesus are supposedly in doubt.

Kreeft observes that "most modernist biblical criticism has *not* been scientific and objective, as it claims to be. It almost always approaches the text with *a priori* religious dogmas and unquestioned assumptions in mind, notably, the disbelief of miracles. From the psychological point of view the modernist reconstruction of the texts seems suspiciously like fudging the data to fit the *a priori* theory, altering the evidence, doctoring the tapes."

James R. Edwards, chair of the department of religion and philosophy at Jamestown College, suggests that such "ideological suppositions hardened into dogmatism succeed in overriding historical evidence, fulfilling Shakespeare's dictum that 'thinking doth make it so.' "

Despite the best efforts of the Jesus Seminar panelists and others, however, the scriptural view of Jesus Christ has continued to prevail. Why?

In his best-selling book, *Mere Christianity,* C. S. Lewis writes: "I am trying here to prevent anyone saying the really foolish thing that people often say about Him: 'I'm ready to accept Jesus as a great moral teacher, but I don't accept His claim to be God.' That is the one thing we must not say. A man who was merely a man and said the sort of things Jesus said would not be a great moral teacher. He would either be a lunatic—on the level with a man who says he is a poached egg—or else he would be the Devil of Hell. You must make your choice. Either this man was, and is, the Son of God: or else a madman or something worse."

Lewis continues: "You can shut Him up for a fool, you can spit at Him and kill Him as a demon; or you can fall at His feet and call Him Lord and God. But let us not come with any patronising nonsense about His being a great moral teacher. He has not left that open to us. He did not intend to."

So, what did Jesus intend to say about himself? And why does it matter?

Paul Little observed that "everything about Christianity is determined by the person and work of Jesus Christ. Christianity owes its life and character in every detail to Christ. Its teachings are teachings about Him. He was the origin and will be the fulfillment of its hopes. He is the source of its ideas, which were born of what He said and did."

How is this different from other wisdom traditions? Little made this distinction: "Christianity is what God has done for man in seeking him and reaching down to help him. Other religions are a matter of man seeking and struggling toward God."

Rabbi Harold Kushner sees another interesting and important difference: "In most religions, the people, the community, existed first, and the religion grew out of the people's efforts to understand and sanctify the world." But "Christianity is the most notable exception to this rule: The idea existed before the community did, and people became Christians by accepting the idea, which is why statements about God are more prominent in Christianity than in most other world religions."

What is the central idea of Christianity?

WHAT CHRISTIANS BELIEVE

According to *Time,* "some 1.5 billion Christians around the globe [celebrate] the Passion and Resurrection of their Lord, who died on the Cross for their sins and rose again on the third day." That idea is what Christians refer to as the good news—the gospel of Jesus Christ.

More than one out of every four people alive today professes some degree of allegiance to those truth claims. No other group—except "women" and "men"—lays claim to such a sizable proportion of the world's population.

What exactly do Christians believe?

First, Christians believe in *Christmas.* That is, that when Jesus was conceived by the Holy Spirit in the Virgin Mary's womb, and born nine months later, God himself entered human history.

How radical is the idea behind Christmas? Domenico Grasso writes that the religious leaders at that time "could not bring themselves to admit that the Almighty, who had created heaven and earth, could have assumed such weakness or that the Infinite would have degraded Himself to the form of a man limited in time and space."

Yet the Scriptures clearly foretold this. Among other things, the prophet Isaiah foretold that the Christ, the Messiah, would be born of a virgin and be called "Immanuel" (literally, "God with us," Isaiah 7:14) and "Wonderful Counselor, Mighty God, Everlasting Father, Prince of Peace" (Isaiah 9:6b).

Furthermore, the angel of the Lord told Joseph, the Messiah's adoptive father: " 'Joseph son of David, do not be afraid to take Mary home as your wife, because what is conceived in her is from the Holy Spirit. She will give birth to a son, and you are to give him the name Jesus, because he will save his people from their sins' " (Matthew 1:20b–21).

What must this incarnation have felt like for God?

Philip Yancey writes: "Imagine for a moment becoming a baby again: giving up language and muscle coordination, and the ability to eat solid food and control your bladder. God as a fetus! Or imagine yourself becoming a sea slug—that analogy is probably closer. On that day in Bethlehem, the Maker of All That Is took form as a helpless, dependent newborn."

Christian statesman Leighton Ford notes: "We must constantly remind ourselves of [Archbishop of Canterbury] William Temple's great statement that 'Christianity is the most materialistic of the world's great religions,' or as C. S. Lewis has it, 'God loves material things. He made them!' The doctrine of creation and incarnation drive home the truth that God is 'down to earth.' He made our bodies, He saw that they were good. Christ came 'in the flesh.' "

Second, Christians believe in *Good Friday.* That is, that after three or four years ministering throughout Palestine, Jesus Christ told his disciples that they were going to Jerusalem, where he would be arrested, "convicted" that same night in an illegally assembled kangaroo court (on charges that he was claiming falsely to be the Messiah), and crucified on a Roman cross.

How radical is the idea behind Good Friday? The New Testament records that when Jesus explained it, "The disciples did not understand any of this. Its meaning was hidden from them, and they did not know what he was talking about" (Luke 18:34). It went completely against their hopes and dreams for the Messiah.

Yet the prophet Isaiah wrote at length foretelling that, as a man, the Christ would be beaten and pierced, dying for the sins of the people. In the middle of this Messianic passage, Isaiah wrote: "We all, like sheep, have gone astray, each of us has turned to his own way; and the LORD has laid on him the iniquity of us all" (Isaiah 53:6).

What kind of savior willingly gets himself killed? Jesus explained to his disciples beforehand: "I lay down my life—only to take it up again. No one takes it from me, but I lay it down of my own accord. I have authority to lay it down and authority to take it up again" (John 10:17b–18).

What was his motivation? To bring people into a right relationship with God by paying the penalty for their sins, granting them the promise of eternal life, making them part of God's family forever, and giving them free access to God through prayer.

Peter said of Jesus, "He himself bore our sins in his body on the tree, so that we might die to sins and live for righteousness; by his wounds you have been healed. For you were like sheep going astray, but now you have returned to the Shepherd and Overseer of your souls" (1 Peter 2:24–25).

Jesus himself said he didn't come "to condemn the world, but to save the world" (John 3:17). To save it, that is, from sin, death, and God's judgment.

Third, Christians believe in *Easter.* That is, that after three days in a borrowed tomb Jesus Christ rose from the dead, appeared to his disciples repeatedly over a period of forty days, then met together with hundreds of followers before ascending back to heaven.

Paul explained the good news this way: "For what I received I passed on to you as of first importance: that Christ died for our sins according to the Scriptures, that he was buried, that he was raised on the third day according to the Scriptures, and that he appeared to Peter, and then to the Twelve. After that, he appeared to more than five hundred of the brothers at the same time" (1 Corinthians 15:3–6a).

How radical is the idea behind Easter? Even though the Jewish religious leaders, Roman officials, and Jesus' own disciples knew he had said he would rise again "on the third day," no one expected he would fulfill that prophecy literally. When his disciples first heard from reliable witnesses that Jesus had risen from the dead, they couldn't believe it. When Jesus first appeared to them, in the upper room, they were frightened.

"A thing is not necessarily true," Oscar Wilde wrote, "because a man dies for it." Yet Jesus Christ validated his message by rising from the dead.

"To die for an idea," wrote Anatole France, "is to place a pretty high price upon conjecture." Yet Jesus' disciples—to a man—were willing to lay down their lives as eyewitnesses to his resurrection.

According to a *Newsweek* cover story: "By any measure, the resurrection of Jesus is the most radical of Christian doctrines. His teachings, his compassion for others, even his martyr's death—all find parallels in other stories and religious traditions. But of no other historical figures has the claim been made persistently that God has raised him from the dead."

The astounding thing is, the religious leaders and Roman officials were at a loss to disprove the resurrection of Jesus Christ from the dead. They started a rumor that the disciples had stolen the body. But that body—very much alive—kept up a very busy itinerary for nearly six weeks, first in Jerusalem and later in the region of Galilee.

Formerly frightened disciples were transformed, almost overnight, into bold witnesses to Jesus Christ's resurrection and offer of eternal life to all who would believe.

Grasso writes of the attractiveness of the Christian message: "If one conceives of faith as an encounter of love between man and God, the whole history of salvation, all divine teaching, is easily understood. God has first loved us and demonstrated this love by His works, including the greatest of them all, the gift of His only-begotten Son (John 3:16). Then He has asked us to reciprocate. The invitation to the love of God from all the facts of sacred history seems to spring as St. John has expressed so happily in his first letter, 'Let us therefore love, because God first loved us' (1 John 4:19)."

Grasso further describes the attractiveness of Jesus: "Christ is the synthesis of all values which man needs and to which he aspires. . . . [T]he man who loves beauty, truth, beatitude, justice and eternal life is spontaneously attracted by Christ, who incarnates these realities within Himself. The attraction is spontaneous and leaves man perfectly free."

This assumes, of course, that Jesus truly was (and is) God-become-man. Not everyone is willing to concede that point. But that is precisely the point I'm trying to make.

To truly experience Jesus Christ's divinity, one has to believe what the apostle Paul wrote: ". . . there is one God and one mediator between God and men, the man Christ Jesus, who gave himself as a ransom for all men" (1 Timothy 2:5–6a).

ONE OF US?

"So what if God was one of us?" sings Joan Osborne in the catchy tune off her popular "Relish" album. What if God did become one of us? How would God be like us? How would God be different? How would we even know?

I believe that, in Jesus, God *did* become one of us. God incarnate shared a common name with thousands of other Jewish boys—and for all practical purposes remained a stranger. For thirty years almost no one outside Nazareth knew him, let alone grasped his divine identity.

To be certain, Jesus' manner and character impressed many in his town. He epitomized the Jewish ideals of truthfulness, wisdom, reverence, and love. But no one outside a small circle—by A.D. 25 perhaps only his widowed mother—knew he was God become flesh.

Shortly after turning thirty years of age, however, Jesus embarked on a most difficult task—revealing his true identity to a people long convinced that God is in his heaven, period.

To the transcendence of God, Jesus revealed God's desire for immanence—nearness to us. How much closer could he have come than by becoming one of us?

Not one of us in the usual sense of the word—only human. Rather, one of us in the best sense—human, yet divine. Perfect. Without sin, yet full of emotion. Fully God and at the same time fully man.

I reject the misconception popular in certain pseudoreligious circles that Jesus was passionless, mild, weak. How pathetic—and how utterly unsupported by the earliest historical records, which paint vivid pictures of Jesus' emotions.

Here is a man who loves and rebukes, who laughs and cries. In every circumstance, he plays the part and plays it well. Far from a caricature, we see Jesus four-dimensionally, fully alive in time-space.

Again, this idea is the opposite from that of all other religions. Instead of man searching (in vain) for the God of eternity, God searches for man in time. According to Kreeft, the God of the Bible is "the Hound of Heaven, the divine lover, the Father looking for his prodigal son, the shepherd for his lost sheep." Always knocking on our heart's door. Always seeking entrance into our lives.

Kreeft writes that, at every turn in the Scriptures, "God always takes the initiative, from the act of Creation on. The supreme example is the Incarnation, the supreme example of taking history and time and the created world seriously. Instead of the passive Eastern God receiving man's search, man's spiritual efforts, Jesus is himself the Western God barging into man's world physically."

Bigger than myth, Jesus made his identity the point of every miracle, every teaching. Why? Because if he truly was (and is) God, someday every knee will bow and every tongue will confess that Jesus Christ is Lord (Philippians 2:10–11).

Not surprisingly, many people have sought to remake Jesus in their (less than divine) image: Jesus as enlightened teacher, Jesus as New Age mystic, Jesus as black Messiah, Jesus as patron saint of Marxist revolutionaries.

Cuban president Fidel Castro says, "I've always considered Christ to be one of the greatest revolutionaries in the history of humanity." I couldn't have said it better, but I doubt Castro and I have the same thing in mind.

Jesus wasn't a prototypical Marxist-Leninist. He had no desire to overthrow the oppressive Roman Empire by force. Yet the Jesus of the Bible can revolutionize your life; he revolutionizes a city or nation when enough people embrace him. History bears that out, and I've seen it with my own eyes in parts of Latin America, Europe, and Asia.

Jesus wasn't simply a first-century wonder-worker, either. Henk Kamsteeg makes this clear: "God is not David Copperfield. He doesn't do magic shows. Jesus' earthly miracles were pointed and purposeful because they were all related to the kingdom."

In his gospel, St. John calls these miracles "signs." Signs of what? That Jesus is truly God-become-man. Signs of God's mercy and power. Signs that demanded a response: do you believe Jesus is God-become-man, or not? (If you still have questions, I recommend that you read John's gospel for yourself.)

I also recommend that you tell God, in your heart, in your own words:

"God, if you exist—and I don't know that you do—and if you can hear this prayer—and I don't know if you can—I want to tell you that I am an honest seeker after truth.

"Show me if Jesus is your Son and the only Savior of the world. And if you bring conviction to my mind, I will trust him as my Savior. I will follow him as my Master and I will obey him as the King of my life. I will join your church and love your sons and daughters."

What will your response be?

OUR RESPONSE TO JESUS?

When it comes to responding to Jesus, I find it's important to distinguish between *reverence, religion,* and *relationship.*

The French emperor Napoleon Bonaparte, for instance, appeared to revere God's Son: "I know men; and I can tell you that Jesus Christ is no mere man." Yet Napoleon concluded that "All religions have been made by men" and didn't have much use for most of them. Nothing I've read suggests that Napoleon professed to truly know or love God.

The unique hallmark of the Judeo-Christian heritage is its emphasis on relationship. Both Testaments describe biblical characters in terms of whether or not God is with them, and whether or not they wholeheartedly love God.

Nowhere in the Scriptures does anyone ever muse, "Is God relevant?" It's simply assumed if God is with you, if you love God with all your heart, that makes all the difference in the world.

Consider the historical accounts of Abraham, Isaac, Jacob, Joseph, Moses, Joshua, Ruth, Samuel, David, Solomon, Isaiah, Jeremiah, and the rest of the Old Testament heroes of the faith. Consider the stories of Peter, James, John, Mary, Paul, and the rest of the New Testament heroes. Without exception, the successes and failures of every biblical character are directly linked by the Scriptures to their relationship with God (or lack thereof).

Like Napoleon, many miss this crucial point. It's not enough to revere the great religious leaders of the past. It's not even enough to become an active member of one of the world's great religions.

Why is it so important to love God? In part, because out of that relationship flows a genuine, heartfelt, sacrificial love for others. Our lives become better *now,* not just in eternity.

You may be thinking, "But surely Jesus isn't the only way to know and love God?" Again, aren't there other options?

David Manning White contends, "When Jesus of Nazareth observed, 'There are many mansions in my Father's house,' was he not telling us that God's essential message is always the same, and that the diverse ways that mankind perceive it are not of ultimate importance?"

No. That's not what Jesus had in mind at all, for he goes on to say, in the very same paragraph, "I am the way and the truth and the life. No one comes to the Father except through me" (John 14:6).

The late Richard Halverson, chaplain of the United States Senate for many years, once noted: "Jesus Christ remains as always the central issue in history. . . . Every other issue in history is secondary to the eternal issue of man's salvation."

Why? Because if Jesus was telling the truth, he alone provides what this world is looking for—hope, peace, security, forgiveness, meaning, dignity, purpose, and the assurance of eternal life.

Is someone knocking at your conscience's door?

Are you going to listen—and respond?

Let me explain how in the next chapter.

DAVID'S STORY

God is relevant—even if your experience in the Church has left a bitter aftertaste in your mouth.

Growing up, David felt like a sleepwalker. He went to church regularly, even though he didn't really believe in God. Still, he kept going through the motions, Sunday after Sunday, mostly out of respect for his extended family.

"Sometimes at the end of a particularly pointed sermon I would feel a twinge, a suspicion that the whole business of Christianity was true and that I ought to heed its message," David later wrote. "But I spurned 'altar calls,' justifying my inaction with a private little list of reasons:

"1. I was wary of falling into traps, especially those laid by persuasive speakers; I was not about to let myself be taken in by a mere speech, not even a convincing one.

"2. I was deterred by my distaste for 'churchianity'—a distaste I extended to Christianity itself.

"3. I reasoned that I had years and years ahead of me, plenty of time for making decisions.

"4. I argued that it would be too lazy for me, a product of a Christian environment, merely to accept the faith of my parents.

"The latter thought prompted me to seek out a book on comparative religions. After reading it, I dropped the subject entirely. That was the extent of my great intellectual search."

One Sunday, our paths crossed when I spoke at David's church. One statement caught his attention: a person can't live right until he or she has settled the basic issue of life, his or her relationship with God. David knew he hadn't settled that issue.

Over the course of several months, God brought several friends into David's life who spoke convincingly of the transforming power of faith in God through Jesus Christ. One of those friends, Bernice, recommended that David read *Mere Christianity* by C. S. Lewis.

David wrote: "For the first time I began to see the truth that had surrounded me all my life as water surrounds a fish. I began to see myself in my true position—as a creature beneath his Creator. I saw the validity of Jesus' claim to be the Son of God, the sin of continuing to disbelieve that claim, and the absurdity of letting all my little objections stand in the way of trusting in the Creator of the universe."

So, on a bright, clear morning, sitting in his car, this intelligent, promising college student prayed to God and received Jesus Christ as his Savior.

"All was quiet," he later remembered. "There was no drama, no warm feeling, no 'Hallelujah Chorus' in the sky—only relief, and the assurance that at that very moment, far off in the unimaginable reaches of heaven, my name was being written in the Book of Life."

After finishing college, David wrote about his conversion experience and spoke in a remarkable way about his anticipation of spending eternity with God.

A year later, at age twenty-six, David died—young, to be sure, but confident of heaven.

CHAPTER 7

YES TO GOD?

You have a choice to make.

If someone walked up right now, as you're reading this book, and asked whether you had decided to believe in God through Jesus Christ yet, how would you respond?

Would you say, *"Yes, I think I do believe. I believe the Lord is knocking on the door of my soul. I'm ready to invite him in"*? Or, *"No, I have my reasons not to trust Jesus Christ, at least not yet. Who knows? Maybe Nietzsche and the others were right. What does Palau know"*? Or some other answer, perhaps?

Would you have said the same thing a week ago? Will you be saying the same thing a week from now?

The faith of most people rises and falls; it's rarely constant. Evelyn Waugh used to say faith is a voyage of discovery. Another writer has said: "No man is entirely religious. Religious men have their doubts. Likewise no man is always an atheist. Atheists have their moments of faith."

The purpose of this book isn't to erase all doubts but to make sure you and I don't sleepwalk through life without wrestling with one of the most important of all life's questions: What is my response to God?

It's not a matter of simply thinking the right thoughts but—as Peter Kreeft reminds us—"choosing to answer the door and let God into our life, as He so desires, on His terms, not ours."

WHAT DO YOU BELIEVE?

I realize not everyone wants to meet God on his terms.

A majority of Americans claim to embrace at least some classic Christian beliefs. But pick-and-choose syncretism has crept even into the Church.

Seven out of every ten Americans, for instance, say they believe in the God of the Bible. The other thirty percent embrace unorthodox definitions of God, including "Everyone is God" and "God represents a state of higher consciousness."

While most Americans believe Jesus Christ is the Son of God, forty-two percent believe that when he lived on earth "Jesus Christ was human and committed sins, just like other people." How terrible and contrary to the facts. Yet that's what some of us think.

Nearly forty percent of Americans believe Jesus Christ is the only way to eternal salvation, almost fifty percent believe everyone shares the same fate, and a majority believe a person who is "good enough" will go to heaven.

At least on that last bastion of orthodoxy, nearly half of the Americans who claim to be Christians embrace *un*orthodox, heretical doctrines.

Could the problem be that some who claim to be Christians don't even know what makes someone a Christian?

Thomas Oden, professor of theology and ethics at Drew University, has spoken out against the rather cozy idea that religion is "gathering around the center" (Lewis Mudge's phrase), as if the core of religious ideology doesn't require circles of definition.

"Can there be a center without a circumference?" asks Oden. Without a circumference, he says, a center "is just a dot, nothing more. Without boundaries a circle could not be a circle. If the circle of faith is seeking to identify its center, it cannot do so without identifying its margins and perimeters."

Oden further states, "To proclaim generously that anyone's truth is as valid as anyone else's truth is to deny the existence of truth altogether."

When it comes to "gathering around the center" of Christianity, seventeen of twenty Americans consider themselves "Christians." But when it comes to drawing a circumference around Christianity, Americans either refuse to try or, more likely, they hold one or more popular cultural myths about what makes someone a Christian:

- being born in America
- thinking positively
- living a good life
- going to church
- giving to others
- getting baptized
- taking communion
- believing in God
- talking about Jesus
- speaking in tongues
- praying to God
- reading the Bible

Does it matter which of these popular myths you believe? Or whether you dismiss them all and instead advocate determining what makes someone a Christian by biblical revelation?

To paraphrase Oden, "Yes!"

Without a circumference defining what makes someone a "Christian," anyone can claim the label. More than 200 million Americans do.

No wonder Oden decries the "persistent illusion of compulsive hypertolerationism," claiming that a "community of faith with no boundaries can neither have a center nor be a community."

The contemporary crisis of definition within popular American evangelicalism mirrors, in part, a much longer-standing question of what defines classic Christianity.

Admittedly, I am often criticized—sometimes vehemently—for seeking to define and proclaim the classic Christian message. This book isn't meant to be a response to such criticisms. Abraham Lincoln said it well:

"If I were to try to read, much less answer, all the attacks made on me, this shop might as well be closed for any other business. I do the very best I know how—the very best I can; and I mean to keep doing so until the end.

"If the end brings me out all right, what is said against me won't amount to anything. If the end brings me out wrong, ten angels swearing I was right would make no difference."

If the classic Christian message is true, however, who would not feel compelled to do everything he or she could, by all available means, to communicate its life-changing message to others? That alone motivates the writing of this book.

Please, hear what I'm saying. I'm writing this book because I believe in its message with all my heart, not in some romantic attempt to defend the faith of my European forefathers (who were agnostics at best, although my dad did turn to God before his death).

I realize the Christian "faith" of many people has more to do with heredity, culture, and geography than with doctrine or heart-felt love for God. But dare we neglect the latter?

Although I believe in God, one by one each of my four sons had to choose whether to embrace him too. For years, my son Andrew said no. It broke my heart, he experienced untold grief, but the choice was his.

My concern is that most people don't even know there's a choice to be made. In the closing chapter of his autobiographical book,

Self-Consciousness, novelist John Updike writes: "Of my own case, looked at coldly, it might be said that, having been given a Protestant, Lutheran, rather antinomian Christianity as part of my sociological make-up, I was too timid to discard it. My era was too ideologically feeble to wrest it from me, and Christianity gave me something to write about, and a semblance of a backbone, and a place to go on Sunday mornings, when the post offices were closed."

In *New Criterion,* reviewer Brooke Allen writes: "Protestantism is [Updike's] creed of choice not because he believes its doctrines to be truer or the way of life it enjoins more perfect, but because it happens to be the manifestation of the religious impulse that is specific to his own country and century."

Christianity of this variety is nominal at best. It may potentially do some good but—if they were here today—the apostles of atheism likely would charge it with great harm. It's a poor imitation of the real thing.

ARE YOU A REAL CHRISTIAN?

When *Time* magazine and other sources speak of 1.5 billion to 1.7 billion Christians worldwide, that sounds impressive—until you subtract those who lack a genuine, vibrant relationship with God.

Perhaps the most famous "Christians" I've met include the presidents, prime ministers, and royalty of various "Christian" nations around the world.

People from non-Western nations, including my well-educated neighbor from India, traditionally view such heads of Western nations as the leading representatives of Christianity. That's not always the case, of course.

At one rather formal dinner, I was seated next to a member of European royalty. If you had asked anyone in the country if she were a Christian, they would have stared at you for a moment, then replied, perhaps curtly, "Of course Her Royal Highness is."

Yet during the course of that dinner, this princess asked me how she might know with certainty that she had eternal life. Even though she represents one of history's most notably religious nations and unhesitantly claimed to be a Christian, she had never embraced a personal relationship with Jesus Christ.

That evening, I explained she had to make a choice, a choice the Bible says we're all invited to make. That choice is to humble ourselves before God and in prayer:

- tell God that we believe in the good news (gospel) of Jesus Christ—all that Christmas, Good Friday, and Easter really mean.
- repent of our sins and ask God for his free gift of salvation—complete forgiveness of sins, an absolutely cleansed conscience, a new heart, God's indwelling presence, eternal life, and a warm welcome into God's family forever.

Later, I received a note from this princess, confirming that she had prayed to receive Jesus Christ into her heart and life and now had the assurance of salvation. She was so happy to be at peace with God. She was overjoyed to be experiencing his power at work within her.

Over the years, I've received tens of thousands of such letters. The longer individuals wait to write, I find, the longer the letters tend to be—telling of all God has done in their lives since the day they committed their lives to him.

One rather wealthy British young man wrote to say:

"I wanted to live my life my way and did not want God interfering in it. The Lord honored my arrogance and allowed me to go my own way but such is His grace and mercy that although I had turned my back on Him, He did not turn His back on me.

"Going my own way, I made quite a mess of my life and indulged myself with most of the things young men get up to, drinking liquor, swearing, and blaspheming my way through each day. In addition, I worshipped money and hoarded considerable quantities of it; I had no love or respect for people and in particular loathed children.

"Part of me must still have been reaching out for God, however, because I saw your [British Broadcasting Corporation] programme advertised in the newspaper and resolved to watch it, not having much idea what to expect.

"As I watched the programme that evening, I felt something saying to me very powerfully, 'You must listen to what this man is saying,' and I do not think I could have left that television set if the room had caught fire!

"I was utterly convinced of the truth of all I saw and heard in that programme and the following day I sincerely prayed a prayer of commitment to Jesus Christ.

"I started attending a church here and the Lord freed me of my love of money. He replaced this with a love of people and also of children. I now help in the running of a youth club and many other Christian activities which would have been inconceivable for me only two years ago.

"In addition, I have been baptised and have many Christian friends whom I love very dearly."

A while later, I heard from a young woman who works as a television production assistant:

"By the time I was about to leave college to go out into the big wide world, God was nowhere on my list of priorities. As I had to decide what to do with my life, a voice inside me kept saying, *You're going to work for the BBC* (at the time I did not realize this voice was God!).

"So, because this thought just wouldn't go away I applied for a job as a secretary in the BBC and sure enough they gave me a job. The day I started work at the BBC in London I met a girl there who was a committed Christian and she became my best friend. What's more, the office in which I was placed looked directly out onto All Souls Church.

"Well, after working at the BBC for two months my friend invited me to hear a speaker at All Souls Church, so out of kindness to her I went along. Luis Palau was the speaker, and as he spoke I felt God was calling me to change. But at the end of the meeting I left the church firmly resolved in my mind that I was quite happy with my life—my job, my boyfriend, and competing in long distance running—and I didn't want God to come and ruin things.

"One day six months later, the same kind of voice that had said, *You're going to work for the BBC,* said, *You must go and listen to this chap in All Souls again.* He had now come back for a massive Mission to London. So this time I asked my Christian friend to come because I'd already decided I was going!

"I knew it was time to stop running away from God. So at the end of the meeting I opened my heart to Jesus. I can't explain the joy I felt in my heart, but I know when I walked out of the church I was a changed person—I loved Jesus and wanted to follow Him.

"Since I gave my life to Jesus, He turned it upside down and has sometimes allowed me to go through some very hard things but I know I've found the real reason for living—knowing Jesus."

In a sense, this book is my own testimony of faith. Its publication comes almost exactly fifty years since I came to belief in God and, more specifically, in Jesus Christ as my Lord and Savior.

Every person's story is different, but "there arrives a moment in every person's life in which he . . . takes a position regarding his destiny, deciding either for good or for bad, either for or against God," Domenico Grasso once observed.

Billy Graham said, "There is no more urgent and critical question in life than that of your personal relationship with God and your eternal salvation." I certainly felt that urgency when I committed my life to Christ.

Have you decided for or against God yet?

C. S. Lewis said: "There is no neutral ground in the universe: every square inch, every split second is claimed by God and counterclaimed by Satan." Bob Dylan said it a bit more succinctly: "It might be the Devil or it might be the Lord, but you've got to serve somebody."

Sadly, the longer one puts off a decision for God, the harder it gets. Psychoanalyst Erich Fromm once wrote: "Our capacity to choose changes constantly with our practice of life. The longer we continue to make the wrong decisions, the more our heart hardens; the more often we make the right decisions, the more our heart softens—or better perhaps, comes alive."

This book is an invitation for you to come alive to God. You can do so right now, before another hour goes by.

What are you waiting for?

MANDY'S STORY

Mandy was thirteen when I met her following a youth rally outside London.

Mandy told me her father, a famous jazz musician, and her mother, a well-known British television personality, were divorced. They never attended church, never talked about God, and didn't even own a Bible.

Mandy said she had never heard about Jesus Christ. But when she learned that Jesus died for her sins on a Roman cross, rose again, and was coming back to take all those who believed in him to heaven, she prayed with me and invited Jesus into her heart.

As we neared the end of our discussion, I showed her what Jesus says to all believers in John 10:28: "I give them eternal life, and they shall never perish; no one can snatch them out of my hand."

She said, "That's what I've got."

As the months passed, Mandy began to tell others what Jesus Christ had done for her. She told her family and her school friends that she knew for certain she was going to heaven when she died.

Three years later the phone call came. Mandy had gone on a date three days before her sixteenth birthday, the voice on the other end told me. It had begun to drizzle and the car swerved out of control and crashed. Mandy's date was thrown clear of the convertible and was uninjured.

But Mandy died instantly.

Mandy's parents asked me to "give the sermon" at her funeral service because, they said, "Mandy talked about nothing more than Jesus, Luis Palau, and going to heaven."

On the day of the funeral, the church was filled with famous personalities, all of whom had a view of the casket that contained Mandy's body.

"Ladies and gentlemen," I said to these famous people, "what you see in the casket is not Mandy. It is Mandy's body, but the real Mandy is not here. Mandy is in heaven with Jesus Christ because the Bible says, 'away from the body and at home with the Lord' " (2 Corinthians 5:8).

Then I said to them, "We're going to bury Mandy's body this afternoon. But the Bible says that the body is just the house of the soul and spirit, the essence of who we really are. Because Mandy had eternal life, she went straight to heaven when she died. Although her body will stay here, her soul and spirit went immediately to be with the Lord."

Compared to eternal life, all other decisions aren't that important when you think about it. Lewis wrote: "No one is ready to live life on earth until he is ready for life in heaven." We don't normally think about it that way, but it's true.

Mandy was prepared for her trip into eternity. Are you? Our journey on earth may last seventy, eighty, or ninety years, or it may end without warning. We need to be ready!

WHAT ABOUT YOU?

Suppose you were to die tonight and, upon arriving at the gate of heaven, the Lord asked you, "Upon what basis do you request entrance into my heaven?"

Perhaps your answer would be, "I confess I'm not perfect. I've mistreated lots of people, as well as myself. But I've done some good as well, Lord. Doesn't that count for something?"

Or maybe you would answer, "Lord, I wasn't too bad. I didn't murder anyone or cheat on my spouse. My children didn't end up in jail, and I was promoted to vice-president of my company because of my honesty and hard work."

Either way, the Lord would have to answer, "Good works are good, but not good enough. No one who is impure in any way can enter here." The only way God will allow us into heaven is if we accept the forgiveness he has provided for us through his Son, Jesus Christ, as Mandy did.

Jesus paid for our sins by his blood given on the cross, and we can live eternally with him in heaven because he conquered death. God loves us so much, he sacrificed his own Son so we could live with him forever. But you must respond, you must make a choice. You must "confess with your mouth, 'Jesus is Lord,' and believe in your heart that God raised Him from the dead" to be saved (Romans 10:9).

Have your sins been forgiven? Or maybe you think you can get to heaven on your own? The good works you have done will never be good enough. The Bible says, "All our righteous acts are like filthy rags" (Isaiah 64:6). They are useless to save your soul and get you to heaven. God wants us to do good works, but not because they will save us.

Unless you have Jesus Christ in your heart as your Savior, you do not have eternal life. You may do many good things: attend church, give money to the poor, even read the Bible, but that will not get you into heaven.

God says we cannot earn a place in heaven. Eternal life is a gift he gives us when we trust in Christ. "For it is by grace you have been saved, through faith—and this not from yourselves, it is the gift of God—not by works, so that no one can boast" (Ephesians 2:8–9).

Are you ready to accept God's gift of eternal life in heaven? If you make that choice, the Bible teaches Jesus Christ will come into your heart, you will become a child of God, your sins will be forgiven, and you will be spotless in the eyes of the holy God. He will say to you, "Welcome! Welcome to my family! I have a house ready for you in heaven, and you will live with me for eternity."

How do you trust God? How can you express that inner choice? By praying a simple prayer of faith, like this one:

"Thank you, Lord, for preparing a place for me in your heavenly home. Thank you that Jesus Christ died on the cross and took away all my shame and guilt, and forgave all my past, present and future sins by his shed blood. Thank you most of all that Jesus rose from the dead. I believe Jesus is alive today and is reigning as King of kings and Lord of lords. I confess my failure and sins to you. I renounce my evil deeds. Come into my heart, wash me from all my sins, fill me with your presence, and make me your child. I will serve you for the rest of my life until you take me home to heaven and I see you face to face. I will bow before you in heaven as I bow right now here on earth."

The important thing isn't saying the right words but, perhaps for the first time in your life, talking heart to heart with the Lord Jesus Christ and inviting him in.

If you've never done so, I urge you to give your life to God right now, where you're at, in the quietness of your heart.

YOUR TURN

While reading this book, have you invited the Lord Jesus into your heart?

If so, congratulations! Please, write and tell me about your decision. I'll be glad to send you a free book about growing in your newfound Christian faith. It's titled *Your New Life With Christ.* Be sure to ask for it when you write.

We'll also be glad to try to send you the address of a good church in your area. I recommend that you plant your roots deeply in a local church that can help you grow in your relationship with God. *Your New Life with Christ* has more to say about this and other Christian basics.

If you have questions about how God is relevant to your particular situation, write to me as well. My staff and I answer hundreds of such letters each month and we'll be glad to correspond with you.

If you're still undecided about God, keep reading. And then let's dialogue by letter, phone, fax, or e-mail.

I look forward to hearing from you.

Luis Palau
P.O. Box 1173, Portland, Oregon 97207, U.S.A.
Telephone: (503) 614-1500
Fax: (503) 614-1599
E-mail: palau@palau.org
Internet: http://www.gospelcom.net/lpea

Part III

THE PROBLEMS OF THE PAST

Chapter 8

THE DISCIPLES OF DOUBT

It's no secret some people don't want God.

In part, belief in God *feels* old-fashioned. Why would any postmodernist individual choose to embrace God?

Reviewing the writings of some of the most influential thinkers over the past four centuries, it's a miracle anyone believes in God anymore.

As we saw in the first chapter, atheism isn't a new idea. The seeds of the prolific twentieth-century atheistic movement were planted in obscure philosophical God talk during a period of massive changes in seventeenth-century France. Later, they took root in specific attacks against Christianity during the revolutionary nineteenth century in Europe (Chapter 9), and came to fruition through the landmark writings of four of history's most famous atheists (Chapter 10).

Obscure God talk, of course, is an age-old problem. Confucius and Buddha both sidestepped the issue of God in their ancient teachings. Rudyard Kipling was right: "By your silence you shall speak." What they didn't say to their followers proves almost as important as what they did say. To their credit, though, neither philosopher sought to infuse "God" with some new, hitherto unknown meaning, as Plato did.

In Roman times, St. Paul had to warn believers in the city of Colossae, "See to it that no one takes you captive through hollow and deceptive philosophy, which depends on human tradition and the basic principles of this world" (Colossians 2:8) rather than on a true knowledge of God as revealed in the Bible.

Earlier this century, atheist Sigmund Freud rightly complained that many "stretch the meaning of words until they retain scarcely anything of the original sense." Freud was critical of those (especially among his fellow psychoanalysts, such as Carl Gustav Jung) who "give the name of 'God' to some vague abstraction which they have created for themselves."

More recently, philosopher Mortimer Adler has observed: "The whole tenor of human life is affected by whether men regard themselves as supreme beings in the universe or acknowledge a superhuman being whom they conceive of as an object of fear or love, a force to be defied or a Lord to be obeyed. Among those who acknowledge a divinity, it matters greatly whether the divine is represented merely by the concept of God—the object of philosophical speculation—or by the living God whom men worship in all the acts of piety which comprise the rituals of religion."

The tenor of life this past century has been profoundly affected by the speculations of three of Europe's most influential philosophers who hyperinflated "God" to mean almost nothing.

Who were these men, and, out of everything they wrote, what did they say specifically about God?

MARGINALIZING GOD: DESCARTES

The reason we even need to discuss the relevance of God goes back nearly four centuries to the time of René Descartes (1596–1650), often called the father of modern mathematics, the father of modern philosophy, and the father of modern thought.

Descartes lived during a time of massive intellectual paradigm shifts. Suddenly, Aristotelian speculations no longer held sway over the European mind. Medieval Scholastic thought no longer made sense. The sun, moon, the five known planets, and the stars no longer circled the earth.

By 1619, the groundbreaking work of Nicolaus Copernicus, Tycho Brahe, Galileo Galilei, and Johannes Kepler had created an astonishingly new scientific world view. Angry and disillusioned with the old Scholastic school of thought, Descartes sought to chart a new course for humanity.

In many ways, Descartes reminds me of this generation. British writer Jonathan Nicholas, who has lived in America for years, speaks for many when he says, "We don't believe anybody anymore . . . or in anything." Why? Because so much of what he has been told by politicians and public relations practitioners, by reporters and the most popular music stars, hasn't proved to be true.

Nicholas writes: "We're awash on the sea of life and nobody seems to have a moral compass. We need someone to engage us, to embrace us, to fire us with commitment and candor, to fill us with passion, hope and trust. We need, in short, a savior."

With an almost Messianic fervor, Descartes embraced the task of establishing new ideologies. His Christian name, René, meaning *born-again one,* suggests something of the magnitude of his task. In an extraordinary exercise, Descartes decided to doubt everything he could. In his intellectual meditations, this young French philosopher writes of the extreme despair he felt, doubting even his own existence. After what must have been a very troubled night's sleep, Descartes resumed his meditations the next day. In essence, he wondered, "If I am not certain I even exist, what is to save me from unending despair?"

Remembering Archimedes' boast, *"Give me a fixed and immovable point in the universe and I'll move the world,"* Descartes determined to find at least one unquestionably true idea. After much mental wrestling and emotional turmoil, Descartes realized the very fact that he had such troubled thoughts and feelings proved: *"Cognito, ergo sum* (I think, therefore I am)."

From that internal, self-centered fulcrum point, Descartes attempted to build a completely rational philosophy of life. Reminiscent of St. Augustine before his conversion to Christianity, Descartes categorically doubted any ideas that couldn't be logically proved, with mathematical-geometrical precision, in his own mind. Out went the old scientific theories. Out went the old classical writings. Out went the old histories. Out went the old religious ideologies. Descartes completely erased the hard drive of knowledge and began to seek for "clear and distinct" truths.

Alternately accused of being an atheist or skeptic, Descartes himself wrote against "the skeptics, who doubt just for the sake of doubting and affect to be always undecided," for his "whole aim was to reach security, and cast aside loose earth and sand so as to reach rock or clay."

Like Charles Darwin years later, Descartes diligently sought to avoid becoming enmeshed in religious controversies. Nevertheless, critics of Descartes charged that his philosophy would undermine Christianity and lead to atheism. Benedict Spinoza soon confirmed their worst fears, publishing first a book on Cartesian philosophy, then another promoting pantheism over Christianity.

Publicly, Descartes distanced himself from Spinoza, Henricus Regis, and others who used Cartesian philosophy to cast doubt on traditional Christian beliefs. He clearly recognized the danger that some would inevitably misapply his teachings and attack belief in God. He even went so far as to advocate postponing a "clean sweep of all [one's] opinions" until one's "mature age," at which point one must have in hand both rules of methodology and a temporary moral code. Why the latter? To avoid giving in to moral abandonment or pleasure rather than applying one's methodology in pursuit of truth.

In his maturity, living in intellectually "free" Holland, Descartes built a new, elaborate, world view—one that permeates postmodern thought even today. The question then and now is, Was Descartes's world view sound?

No, for at least two reasons.

First, Descartes started with an inadequate, self-centered foundation. We need something more substantial than his assertion, "I think, therefore I am."

Second, Descartes had a faulty, limited methodology. We need something more than mathematical certainty to understand reality. Consider:

- *Mathematics is no longer an absolutely certain science.* For instance, for decades mathematicians have admitted that they are unable to deal with some problems related to the infinite.
- *Many of the most important aspects of life cannot be understood, let alone discussed, mathematically.* Descartes had almost no use for history. Small wonder why: you can't talk about history, let alone depth of relationship, in mathematical terms.
- *The deeper the truth, the less certain it appears.* Everyone knows 2 + 2 = 4, but who cares? If my wife Pat says she loves me, while I can't prove it with mathematical certainty, her statement is significant and meaningful to me, if I take her at her word.

Descartes was a genius. He certainly deserves his due. Yet we fail to learn anything from his life if we don't understand that depth of truth must be embraced in the context of relationship, not privatized mental mathematical calculations.

Given the depth of the truth about the divine, then, how great is the commitment someone must make to know anything about God. And even greater is the commitment someone makes in embracing relationship with God himself!

COUNTERING DESCARTES: PASCAL

Four years before Descartes began espousing his philosophical ideas publicly, the other great seventeenth-century French mathematical-philosophical genius, Blaise Pascal (1623–62), was born.

Pascal was an astounding child prodigy. While still a teenager, he invented and patented the first workable calculating machine—the prototype of today's computers.

Descartes and Pascal were similar in many ways and met on several occasions, but certainly never became friends. The older Descartes, for instance, dismissed sixteen-year-old Pascal's discovery of the "mystic hexagram" as something he must have learned from an older man, and later tried to take credit for the idea behind Pascal's first public barometric experiment.

Unlike Descartes, Pascal was more interested in questions of the moment than with finding some grand theory to explain everything. Still, toward the end of his life, he was making extensive notes for what was to be a large philosophical-theological volume. He died, utterly exhausted, at age thirty-nine, leaving behind a huge assortment of extensive notes written on various-sized sheets, half sheets, and strips of paper. Similar to Muhammad's Koran, Pascal's *Pensées* were collected and published posthumously. Hans Küng says "they have provided mankind with more food for thought than all the solid philosophical and theological manuals of that time."

Descartes wanted to work out truth in his head and only afterward—if he had time—conduct an experiment to prove and confirm it (thus often proclaiming as fact ideas that didn't stand up to empirical verification). Pascal, however, saw experimentation as a much broader, more useful tool for learning. He was quite content to try something, measure the results, and then attempt to determine what they meant.

Descartes valued thinking above all else, but Pascal recognized the broader spectrum of the soul—affection, intuition, and instinct, for instance. Pascal believed, "The heart has its reasons" that go beyond intellectual reasoning. In this, Pascal was a much more modern man—he valued a person of sound head and heart, who consistently lived out what he knew and felt to be true.

Pascal clearly saw the limits of reason: "It is just as pointless and absurd for reason to demand proof of first principles from the heart before agreeing to accept them as it would be absurd for the heart to demand an intuition of all the propositions demonstrated by reason before agreeing to accept them. Our inability must therefore serve only to humble reason, which would like to be the judge of everything, but not to confute our certainty. As if reason were the only way we could learn!"

Furthermore, Pascal saw the limits of Descartes's methodology: "Wisdom is something different from enlightenment, it is different from reasoning. But wisdom is not science, wisdom is an elevation of the soul . . . it reasons little, nor does it proceed mathematically from concepts, through a series of syllogisms, in order to reach what it takes to be the truth . . . but it speaks from the fullness of the heart."

Pascal's distaste of Descartes's *esprit de géométrie* could hardly have been stated more forcefully—though before his death, Pascal penned a brief line, saying he hoped to write a lengthy discourse "against those who probe science too deeply. Descartes."

Like Descartes, however, Pascal was profoundly influenced by the collapse of the old world view. Suddenly, the universe was a much larger, more mysterious place. Pascal felt heaven was much too far away ever to reach, and God was nowhere to be seen. Humanity was a mere speck on the face of a small planet spinning through a seemingly endless expanse. In the midst of this cosmic paradigm shift, Pascal wrote, "The eternal silence of these infinite spaces fills me with dread."

During this period of his life, Pascal wrote about "man's unhappiness," about life's great philosophical questions, and about despair in light of the certainty of each individual's death.

Yet Pascal could also write about humanity's *grandeur* in the midst of *misère,* and why man must look beyond himself for answers to life's greatest questions. In short, "hear from your master your true condition, which is unknown to you. Listen to God."

Doesn't that require a leap of faith? Yes, said Pascal, but it's not a blind leap. Rather, it's a wager well worth taking. As the author of the hitherto unknown but immensely useful law of probability, he knew what he was talking about and framed it in Pascal's Wager.

According to Pascal, we all have a choice. He put the wager this way: "Should a man be in error in supposing the Christian religion to be true, he could not be a loser by mistake. But how irreparable is his loss, and how inescapable is his danger should he err in supposing it to be false."

In other words, *if it appears God is relevant and I actively pursue a relationship with him, what do I risk losing?* Some of that which is temporal. *If, however, I choose to reject the opportunity to get right with God, what are the odds I could suffer great loss?* Probably pretty high.

Simply put, Pascal's Wager says: "Have faith in God. If there is no God, you have lost nothing. But if there is a God, and you have faith in him, you have won eternity and everything else as well."

How did Pascal come to such a conclusion? Four years after Descartes's death, Pascal had a conversion experience. It was a matter of the heart: "It is the heart which perceives God and not the reason. That is what faith is: God perceived by the heart, not by the reason." Not that Pascal suddenly decided to dismiss reason: but reason *alone* could not bring him "joy" and "peace" with God, and with himself.

In contrast to Descartes, Pascal recognized that "reason's last step is the recognition that there are an infinite number of things which are beyond it," and that "submission and use of reason; that is what makes true Christianity."

Pascal went on to say: "in his [Descartes's] whole philosophy he would like to do without God; but he could not help allowing him a flick of the fingers to set the world in motion; after that he had no more use of God."

And "knowing God without knowing our own wretchedness makes for pride. Knowing our own wretchedness without knowing God makes for despair. Knowing Jesus Christ strikes the balance because he shows us both God and our own wretchedness."

Pascal warned that there are "two excesses: to exclude reason, to admit nothing but reason."

In France, however, godless "reason" almost won the day, provoking what became a bloody, short-lived reign of terror one hundred thirty years after Pascal's death. During that bloodbath, Christianity was toppled and an antigoddess raised up in Notre Dame and celebrated with much sexual frenzy. Atheistic neo-paganism became the new political rule, ruthlessly applied by force. Almost overnight, thousands of men and women lost their lives during an endless round of public executions. The revolutionaries eventually started turning on each other. This nightmare reportedly provoked one comrade to cry, "If there is no God, we'll have to invent one."

The results of the horrible and failed French Revolution were dramatically different from those of the American Revolution fourteen years earlier. Why? In part, because of philosophical differences, of course. But also because of the first Great Awakening in the American colonies, led by Jonathan Edwards (later appointed president of Princeton University). Without that awakening of Christian faith, the history of the past two centuries would have looked much different not only in North America but also elsewhere around the world.

The seeds of other revolutions in Europe and Asia, even more horrific than France's, were planted in nineteenth-century Germany (as we'll see in the next two chapters), after much abstract and ultimately useless philosophical speculation by Kant and Hegel.

IMITATING PLATO: KANT

In eighteenth-century Germany, no philosopher gained greater stature than Immanuel Kant (1724–1804). Although Kant never traveled more than eighty-five miles from his Königsberg birthplace, the influence of his dualistic critical philosophy eventually circled the globe.

His most influential works include *Critique of Pure Reason, Critique of Practical Reason,* and *Critique of Judgment.* His prolific and diligent efforts to expound what is known as critical philosophy came in response to what he perceived to be philosophy's impotence for more than two centuries to answer the big questions:

- Does God exist?
- Do we have free will?
- Does the soul live on after death?

In response to those key questions, Kant answered:

- Yes.
- Yes.
- Yes.

Still, to his critical way of thinking, Kant insisted that we cannot know an abstract thing-in-itself. The best we can do is presuppose its existence (which can't be proved) and seek to think clearly about it. Like Plato, Kant believed we can't know God-himself, per se. We can seek to understand what he is like, but our finite minds can't grasp him-in-himself.

Kant had no problem conceding that we can understand the

things of nature. I'm sure he felt he could fully describe and understand everything he saw during his well-timed afternoon walks. But when he returned to his study, he wasn't as interested in studying natural or special revelation as he was in critically thinking through the big questions of life for himself. Exercising his will quite freely, Kant left his big German Bible on the shelf and wrote new books instead. He neglected to consider the supreme source of truth about God, salvation, and eternal life.

As theologian Jürgen Moltmann reminds us, Kant declared that "a religion which, without hesitation, declares war on reason, will not, in the long run, be able to hold out against it." Yet Kant himself might as well have declared war on classic Christianity when he consigned "God" to the abstract, the unknowable, to make way for "faith" and his new system of ethics.

When Kant looked at the starry skies, intrigued though he was, he said he could see no demonstration of the existence of purpose beyond this world. Exactly how the soul lives on after death, he couldn't say. Ironically, Kant apparently had little time to muse on *the* Immanuel, Jesus Christ, or to consider whether in fact the Son of God had come from heaven, taken human form, and by his life, ministry, death, and resurrection revealed and reconciled God-himself to mankind. To Kant, Christ was merely a good moral example.

Without a way to know God-himself, Kant concluded, life was ultimately dissatisfying. He wrote, "Give a man everything he desires and yet at this very moment he will feel that everything is not everything." Paraphrased: everything this world has to offer isn't enough. We were made to enjoy more. Yet Kant couldn't convincingly say what that *more* was, or how to obtain it. His followers remain among us today.

The late author Allan Bloom described the postmodern dilemma this way: "Because we have come to take the unnecessary to be necessary, we have lost all sense of necessity." Many individuals have a hard time identifying—let alone admitting—their greatest needs. Perhaps we are far too easily satisfied with much less than

God intended. Kant wasn't sure: his "God" wasn't quite that down to earth.

MORE ABSTRACT STILL: HEGEL

The next great German philosopher, Georg Wilhelm Friedrich Hegel (1770–1831), likewise sought to wrestle with life's big questions and create a new philosophical system that superseded his predecessors'.

Although he disagreed with Kant on many points, and sought to make many correctives, Hegel continued to advocate abstract, impersonal ideas about God. As he saw it, truth resided in the mind or spirit, not in the material (which galled Karl Marx). Hegel made this absolute mind his ideal, his idol, his "God," and argued that the unfolding of history gradually revealed this spirit.

Rejecting traditional Christianity as old-fashioned and incomplete, Hegel wrote about the "Death of God" nearly a century before Nietzsche's famous pronouncement. He also wrote a critical *Life of Jesus* that went unpublished but anticipated David Friedrich Strauss's monumental work forty years later.

In God's place, Hegel described a new "God," an evolving conceptual ideal which he said would permeate humanity eventually and make sense of all of history. To him, "Pure reason, incapable of any limitation, is the Deity itself."

In attempting to rescue God from the trappings of the Church and the pages of Scripture, then, Hegel made "God" sound strikingly similar to the fulfillment of his grandiose philosophical aspirations. Instead of fashioning an idol of metal or wood or stone, Hegel crafted a "God" to satisfy his own intellectual lusts.

Admittedly, Hegel often wrote over his own head. Dennis J. De Haan reminds us: "A pupil asked the noted philosopher . . . to explain a passage he had written. Hegel read it and said, 'When that was written, there were two who knew its meaning—God and myself. Now, alas! There is but one, and that is God.' "

On another occasion, Hegel is said to have warned someone overawed by his genius: "What comes from myself in my books is false." Yet from where else did it come?

As Hegel himself admitted, his efforts to create a profound ethical system fell short: "Intellectual enlightenment makes people shrewder, but not better. . . . No book on morality, no intellectual enlightenment can prevent evil inclinations from rising up, from becoming rampant."

Philosophers and theologians still argue about Hegel's ultimate intentions. Was he really trying to preserve religion or to dissolve it? Whatever the case, in an effort to make "faith" reasonable, Hegel undermined many people's interest in the God of Christianity.

Hermann Häring notes: "Hegel's God, if thinkable at all, is only thinkable radically and as a totality. In such a conception, however, freedom disappears. Hegel's speculative synthesis marks a kind of Copernican revolution for the status of philosophy, and in this Hegel's theological opponent in Berlin, F. Schleiermacher, is of one mind with him: God must either be thought out absolutely and without reservation or he must be repudiated without reservation. The logic of this choice is consistent, but dangerous."

In the end, no matter how "rational" or "ideal," a speculative "God" ends up being no God at all, as the leading agnostic and atheistic thinkers of the nineteenth century aggressively sought to prove.

KENNETH'S STORY

Even if someone grows up in a Christian family, that doesn't automatically make him a child of God.

One of my sister's sons grew up in a loving home, where God was honored, yet Kenneth never could figure out what all the fuss was about. To him, "God" meant nothing personally.

In rebellion against his parents (and their faith), Kenneth pursued a sexually promiscuous lifestyle during his university years and then a career in the San Francisco Bay area.

Although still a young man, immensely talented and full of promise, Kenneth started struggling with his health. When he didn't get better, doctors at Stanford University Medical Center ran a series of tests. One confirmed Kenneth's worst fears: he had AIDS.

In the foothills of the northern California mountains, Kenneth and I went for a walk. He struggled for each breath, hardly the vigorous youth I had known a few months before.

At first, when we started talking, I wasn't sure what to expect. J. C. A. Gibson writes: "Too frequently . . . the course of theist-atheist polemic has borne a distressing resemblance either to a political debate or to the sort of adolescent squabble portrayed in Ingmar Bergman's *Wild Strawberries* ('There *is* a God!' 'There is *not!*' 'There is *too!*')." That's the last thing I wanted. But reality is reality. It was time to talk now—or never.

To my surprise, Kenneth admitted that one of the first things he thought about, when the doctor told him he had only four to six months to live, was God. Coming face to face with his mortality had shaken him to the core of his being. Suddenly, God wasn't so abstract, so distant, so irrelevant anymore. His "fast" lifestyle no longer made sense. He turned his life over to God, through Jesus Christ, come what may.

I hugged Kenneth and we prayed. He thanked God for the forgiveness of his sins and for the promise of eternal life, in Jesus' name; I thanked God for Kenneth and prayed at length for his final days here on earth.

Out of tragedy came a brief but shining light: a life transformed, content, at peace. A few months later, we buried Kenneth's body and wept. Yet not as those who have no hope.

St. John reminds us: "God has given us eternal life, and this life is in his Son. He who has the Son has life; he who does not have the Son of God does not have life" (1 John 5:11–12).

I often wonder what might have been. It seemed Kenneth's life had only begun to flourish. Then the flower of youth wilted and was no more.

At least it had flourished for a season.

I sometimes think how different the world might have been if, in their youth, Descartes, Kant, Hegel, and their followers had come alive to God through true conversion to Jesus Christ.

Change the life and thinking of less than a dozen men, and the history of the twentieth century would have taken a much different, far better course.

My dream is that you and I, our loved ones, and many others will embrace that better course.

CHAPTER 9

THE CONVERTS OF CYNICISM

Some people will do almost anything to make God look irrelevant.

The seeds of doubt planted by Descartes, Kant, and Hegel—over and against Pascal's Wager (and the writings of other Christian philosophers, to be sure)—took root in specific attacks against belief in God during the revolutionary nineteenth century in Europe.

These attacks against the reliability of the Scriptures, against Jesus Christ, against the idea of God as Creator, and against the Christian religion as a whole, were carried out in the name of modern science and in the pessimistic spirit of pantheism.

ATTACKING GOD'S WORD: STRAUSS

David Friedrich Strauss (1808–74), a contemporary of Charles Darwin, led the first wave of attack against belief in God by asserting that educated men and women had no reason to believe the Scriptures anymore. Why? Strauss alleged that ancient religionists had corrupted the Bible, obscuring any original truth statements.

Taking a supposedly "scientific-literary" approach to the study of the biblical accounts of the life and ministry of Jesus Christ, Strauss compared and contrasted the four gospel accounts, dismissing virtually all of the miracles out of hand, identifying numerous alleged contradictions, and trying to strip each gospel of most of its apparent truth content.

Strauss didn't completely write off the historical value of the gospels: he accepted the crucifixion as historical fact (attested by Tacitus, among others), and spoke of the miracles as "eternal truths"—somehow meaningful, even though they never happened (supposedly).

Strauss's attacks weakened the thunder of Europe's pulpits. Even the most learned clergy faced tough questions about the authority and inspiration of God's word after reading Strauss's two-volume work, *The Life of Jesus, Critically Examined,* which Jesus Seminar panelists and others still cite a century and a half later.

In his infamous work, Strauss sought to remove what he labeled the ancient "myths" about Christ from the historical (gospel) narratives about Jesus. He zealously rejected any ideas of the importance of Jesus outside his homeland over a very short period of time. Instead, Strauss felt the Christological ideals were best ascribed to humanity as a whole. Christology becomes anthropology; humanity, not the Jesus of history, is divine.

By his own authority, then, a nineteenth-century European set himself up as the final authority on ancient Christian history. It's ludicrous, if you think about it.

During a speaking tour in Scotland, I accepted an invitation to a BBC debate with a Glasgow theologian. Like Strauss, this gentleman was a functional atheist, "Christian" in name only. At one point in the debate, I told him rather candidly, "Sir, I can see you don't believe the Bible. So you've put me in a dilemma. Either I have to believe Jesus or I have to believe you. I'll choose Jesus any time." On the air, this "theologian" flew into a fit of anger, calling me every disagreeable name in the book, only underscoring his own lack of credibility.

Not only did Strauss attack Christianity; he later also actively promoted a new way of believing. A contemporary of Strauss said of his book *The Old Faith and the New* that it "is a magnificent expression of the honest conviction of all educated people of the present day who understand this unavoidable conflict between the discredited, dominant doctrines of Christianity and the illuminating, rational revelation of modern science."

In this latter book, Strauss sought to answer various questions:

- Are we still Christians? No.
- Have we still a religion? It depends on what you mean by religion; we have "religious" feelings for the universe.
- What is our conception of the universe? Darwinian.
- Do we believe in the immortality of the soul? No.
- What is our rule of life? We call the shots.

Although wrongly accused of being out-and-out atheists, Strauss and his equally controversial soul mate, Darwin, together launched a tidal wave of agnosticism across Europe.

ATTACKING GOD'S CREATION: DARWIN

News of Strauss's monumental work, *The Life of Jesus, Critically Examined,* reached the ears of British naturalist Charles Darwin (1809–82) during his world-famous voyage aboard HMS *Beagle.*

Ostensibly, Darwin was recruited by Captain Robert FitzRoy to collect scientific evidence supporting the Genesis story of creation. Although offered no salary for his troubles, this young man, who had studied both geology and theology, eagerly accepted this intriguing opportunity to venture around the world. It mattered not that his education was inadequate nor that his scientific equipment was faulty.

Already full of questions before the five-year expedition, Darwin was influenced not only by Strauss but also by Sir Charles Lyell's monumental three-volume work, *The Principles of Geology,* which expounded the theory of uniformitarianism (that existing processes, given enough time, explain the geological results we observe today).

By the time Darwin returned to England he had rejected the ideas that God may intervene in history through miracles and that those who reject God may face eternal punishment in hell. Yet Darwin knew the socioreligious explosiveness of such "heresies" and talked only about his new scientific ideas instead. In fact, Darwin refrained from publishing anything about natural selection and the organic evolution of species until naturalist Alfred Russel Wallace began proposing some of the same ideas that Darwin had been researching for twenty-five years.

By developing the theory of evolution, Darwin provoked a philosophical revolution that still hasn't subsided within Western culture. No other theory has attracted such fervent faith and opinionated opposition within the religious and scientific communities, and among the general populace.

In his own day, Darwin was one of the most popular and most hated men who swore allegiance to the British crown. His world travels and books, including his best-selling work, *On the Origin of Species,* made him an international celebrity.

So great was Darwin's popularity that an atheistic German philosopher residing in London, Karl Marx, requested permission to dedicate a volume of *Das Kapital* to the naturalist. Another atheistic German philosopher, Ludwig Feuerbach, likewise applauded Darwin's writings with enthusiasm. Darwin remained aloof from their endorsements and suggested that, by publishing atheistic propaganda, they might turn the sociopolitical tide against ongoing intellectual freedoms (which was never the case in Protestant nations like Britain, although many atheistic nations later practiced extreme censorship of most political and religious writings).

While Darwin cautiously tried to keep out of the religious controversies lit by his theory, those controversies were fanned into flame by "Darwin's bulldog," Thomas H. Huxley (grandfather of writer Aldous Huxley and geneticist Julian Huxley), by Ernst Haeckel (Germany), Vladimir Kovalevsky (Russia), Asa Gray (United States), and by others.

Often wrongly called an atheist, Darwin at first believed that some sort of deity may have created the first organisms from which other life forms then evolved. Later in life, however, Darwin admitted in his autobiography: "The mystery of the beginning of all things is insoluble by us; and I for one must remain an Agnostic."

The most ardent early Darwinists were definitely atheists, however, often under the guise of pantheism. By the time Darwin was laid to rest in Westminster Abbey, a large percentage of the educated world had accepted evolution as fact, over against the traditional Judeo-Christian belief in God as Creator.

Scientifically, several aspects of Darwin's theory have required correctives, but most of his ideas are still too large to be tested by standard methodology and—some critics say—have been accepted as dogma even though scientists can't prove macro evolution, per se. Not that the scientific community isn't trying to find convincing proofs.

In *Smithsonian* magazine, James Trefil writes: "Only a few years ago, a well-known scientist [Fred Hoyle] said that the odds of life arising anywhere in the Universe are about the same as those that a Boeing 747 will be assembled when a tornado rips through a junkyard." In other words, virtually impossible.

Trefil goes on to say: "But if ideas now circulating in the scientific community turn out to be right, we may find that the occurrence of life isn't nearly as random as we had thought, and indeed may be in a certain sense necessary: life may not be just permitted, but required." Unanswered is the question: *required* by what? Or whom?

PROMOTING PESSIMISM: SCHOPENHAUER

A year after the publication of Darwin's historic book, a then obscure German philosopher named Arthur Schopenhauer (1788–1860) died, content that his newly wrought pessimistic philosophy had brought "comfort" to his soul.

Schopenhauer was a wealthy merchant's son, pessimistic from birth ("Life is a curse of endless craving and endless unhappiness"); abandoned by his father, who apparently committed suicide; and estranged from his mother, who demonstrated little affection for him. He had no use for others, especially women and academicians, and never married. He was lonely, fearful, moody, egocentric ("The world is my idea"), highly critical of others, and obsessively worried about his health.

As an independently wealthy person, thanks to the inheritance his father left him, Schopenhauer was free to do as he wished and found some pleasure in the arts, good food, travel, and occasional amours.

As a young man, Schopenhauer studied the ancient Indian Upanishads, as well as Plato, Kant, and Goethe in university, and later as a nonsalaried lecturer vainly tried to dissuade students from accepting Hegel's abstract philosophical teachings. He was especially impressed with atheistic Buddhism and also with Brahmanism, and talked in glowing terms of the Christian ascetics.

Once while sitting in a Berlin park in a rather melancholic state of mind, this eccentric philosopher was mistaken for a vagrant. The policeman patrolling that neighborhood demanded of Schopenhauer, "Who do you think you are?"

He replied, "I would to God I knew."

In his classic work, *The World as Will and Idea* (which influenced a great many artists, writers, and musicians, including at least two Nobel prize winners—even though, eighteen months after it had been published in 1819, it had sold scarcely one hundred copies), Schopenhauer preached the interrelated virtues of:

- art, especially music, influencing Richard Wagner, among others;
- self-knowledge;
- self-denial, rejecting the will to live—to survive, even to be reincarnated;
- asceticism: developing the moral character to replace self-centeredness with altruism or compassion for others;
- and what Hans Küng describes as "suffering as imposed by fate and often bringing about a complete change of mind."

The goal? Embracing *nothingness* ("nothing" is the last word of his classic work).

In real life, Schopenhauer feared both suffering and death. His pessimistic efforts to overcome those fears apparently succeeded, in the end. Schopenhauer's friend, executor, and later biographer, the lawyer and writer Wilhelm von Gwimmer, talked with Schopenhauer right before Schopenhauer's death.

Gwimmer says Schopenhauer "declared his joy especially in the fact 'that his apparently irreligious teachings "worked as a religion," filled up the place left empty by the loss of faith and became the source of innermost reassurance and satisfaction.' As he passed away, he also declared 'that for him it would be an act of charity to come to absolute nothingness; but death offered no prospect of that. But, however it might be, he had at least a pure *intellectual conscience.*' "

According to Rudolf Zuckerstätter, Schopenhauer's "main significance lies in his original conception of reality and in his compellingly argued and terrifyingly bleak and pessimistic vision of human existence as a meaningless, unceasing, and futile struggle, full of torment and suffering, in a hostile and godless universe."

Is it any wonder that, a few decades later, a generation that thinks of reality and life and God as Schopenhauer did could easily eliminate children in the womb and argue for the destruction of the elderly and feel no compassion for the shooting of unknown persons? For all his talk of "compassion," has Schopenhauer's example moved even one person to true love for his or her fellow human beings?

One of those most influenced by Schopenhauer's pessimistic pseudoreligious philosophy, in the absolutely opposite direction from compassion, was the atheistic philosopher Friedrich Nietzsche, as we'll see in the next chapter.

PROMOTING PANTHEISM: HAECKEL

Following hard and fast in the footsteps of Strauss, Darwin, and Schopenhauer, the atheistic scientist Ernst Haeckel (1834–1919) actively promoted pantheism as a respectable cloak for abandoning belief in God.

Growing up, Haeckel had impressed his family and instructors as a very talented and devout young man. During his university days, however, Haeckel was repelled by the superstitious and repugnant behavior of a group of ignorant Catholic peasants, was influenced significantly by the beliefs of a professor and the writings of Darwin and others, became disillusioned by the tragic death of a good friend, and then disowned Christianity completely when his wife, Anna Sethe, died only a short time after their wedding.

Haeckel promoted, expanded, and in some ways—at least publicly—anticipated Darwin's applications of the theory of evolution to the origin and history of mankind. (One of the more unfortunate applications, promoted by Social Darwinism, sought to justify the inhumane child labor practices in nineteenth-century England.)

Going beyond Darwin, Haeckel completely rejected the divine: "There are no gods or goddesses, assuming that god means a personal, extramundane entity. This 'godless world-system' substantially agrees with the monism or pantheism of the modern scientist."

In turn, Haeckel quoted Schopenhauer with approval: "Pantheism [among Western thinkers of the time] is only a polite form of atheism. The truth of pantheism lies in its destruction of the dualist antithesis of God and the world, in its recognition that the world exists in virtue of its own inherent forces. The maxim of the pantheist, 'God and the world are one,' is merely a polite way of giving the Lord God his *congé.*"

After Strauss and Darwin created a huge wave of agnosticism across the Western world, then Schopenhauer and Haeckel actively promoted pessimistic pseudoreligious ideas freely borrowed in part from Eastern mysticism.

Soon thereafter, the four leading apostles of atheism wrote their antigospels.

ANN'S STORY

Ann's husband, Chuck, returned from a business lunch where I'd spoken, and he told his wife he trusted Jesus Christ as his Savior. Ann's first thought was, "Well, he's under pressure and we're all a little crazy here, so we'll see what happens next."

Ann's and Chuck's lives had begun to fall apart in October 1988. Their daughter had a serious, possibly terminal condition. Six months after first discovering this illness, their son suffered a head injury in a car accident.

By 1992, various medications had left their daughter in a wheelchair. Their son recovered from most of his injuries but had untreatable epilepsy, suffering seizures every five to ten days.

So when Chuck said he wanted to attend church, Ann was all for it. "I was up for anything that would give him peace of mind," she said.

Ann felt she had become a Christian as a child. "My parents didn't go to church, but I went to Vacation Bible School with a friend who asked me," Ann said. "I prayed the prayer at the end of the week, and that was that." She didn't understand the Bible but read many books about religion. The more she read, the more she wanted to know true faith.

So first Ann became Catholic. "I thought that was the best one," she said. "Then I became Jewish, and then I studied religions and thought, 'They're all made up; they're all kind of man-made.' " So Ann became an agnostic.

By the time Ann got to college, she was an out-and-out atheist. Satisfied that her hard work and determination could forge her future, she viewed her Christian friends as smart but weak. She felt "they had this one area where they weren't quite as strong as I was," she said.

The first morning Chuck and Ann attended church, the pastor outlined a clear picture of the Christian life from the apostle Paul's letter to the Romans. He answered Ann's doubts and questions. "Our friends must have told him I was coming," Ann thought.

Then Ann read *Mere Christianity* by C. S. Lewis because she heard he was an atheist, too. "At times I read that book and cried over my ignorance, pride, and stubbornness at how confidently I had rejected this thing I knew nothing about," she said. Yet Ann still didn't lay aside her pride.

When Chuck decided they should join the church, Ann agreed. They attended the membership class. Then Ann found out she had to have "a casual chat" with someone at church to tell them how she came to know Jesus Christ. But she still hadn't trusted Christ. "The Lord knew, 'She needs a deadline—we've got to get going here,' so I had this deadline," she said.

A few hours before Ann was supposed to talk with someone at church, she had lunch with a Christian friend. "That's when I prayed and accepted Christ," she said. "Yet, I didn't have this peace everybody talks about. I was so frightened of this step I had made away from everything I knew before to embrace what I had resisted for so long. Until suddenly I had a sense that someone had His arm around me; I finally had peace.

"What I had thought was my broadminded view of life was really me looking through the wrong end of the telescope."

Chapter 10

THE APOSTLES OF ATHEISM

In the history of ideas, he who shouts the loudest and longest often wins the day.

The "death" of belief in God came to fruition through the landmark writings of four of history's most notorious atheists.

George Bernard Shaw once remarked, "All great truths begin as blasphemies." The great atheists knew this principle well, relentlessly assaulting religious truisms in their effort to espouse new ideas.

The noted atheist Paul Edwards even contends that "the history of heresy, blasphemy, rejection of belief, atheism, agnosticism, humanism, and rationalism," in many respects, also is "the history of the intellectual progress of the human race."

This "progress" led to the annihilation of more than 100 million persons during the past century alone.

THE FATHER OF MODERN ATHEISM: FEUERBACH

The nineteenth-century German philosopher Ludwig Feuerbach (1804–72) is the most famous atheist many people have never heard of. Yet, in many ways, Feuerbach set in motion ideas that have had more impact for evil than any other European philosopher of his day.

Especially through the publication of his materialistic work, *The Essence of Christianity,* Feuerbach made a profound intellectual impact on Karl Marx and his faithful comrade-in-arms Friedrich Engels, among others.

Feuerbach self-confidently declared that he was "the ultimate philosopher pushed to the absolute limit of philosophizing." Drunk on himself, Feuerbach used his writings to invite others to imbibe. Not only that, but (together with Marx and Bruno Bauer) Feuerbach made plans to publish an "Archive of Atheism," while Marx also saw to the French edition of *The Essence of Christianity.*

Born Catholic but raised Protestant, Feuerbach studied to be a minister, "from the standpoint [however] of a rational religiosity." He became disillusioned with Christianity, came under the spell of Hegel (his "second father"), decided to make a name for himself in philosophy, broke with Hegel, and soon thereafter became Europe's most vocal and most insistent atheist.

Feuerbach described his intellectual journey this way: "God was my first thought, reason my second, man my third and last thought." Hans Küng observes that later Feuerbach "had yet a fourth (the sensuous), fifth (nature) and sixth (matter), and committed himself with his notorious proposition 'Man is what he eats [*Der Mensch ist, was er isst*]' to the crude scientific materialism of the 1850s and 1860s."

In doing away with the supernatural and divine, Feuerbach boasted that "humanity can *again* concentrate wholeheartedly on itself, on its world and on the present time. *Instead of* immortal life in a hereafter, a new life here and now; *instead of* immortal souls, capable human beings healthy in mind and body" (emphasis added).

Again? Had this ever worked before? (Feuerbach couldn't say.)

Instead of? Why not both? (Feuerbach wouldn't say.)

After anonymously publishing his first atheistic tract, *Thoughts on Death and Immortality, with an appendix of theological-satirical epigrams,* Feuerbach became the subject of a police inquiry and wrote to his sister: "I am in bad odour, they say I am a horrible freethinker, an atheist, and—as if that were not enough—Antichrist in person."

That publication, and Feuerbach's lack of success as a lecturer, forced him into retirement. Even though he contended he was a philosopher, not a professor of philosophy, Feuerbach tried in vain to apply for professorships at half a dozen universities.

At a mid-life crisis—what to do with the rest of his life—Feuerbach was "rescued" by a wealthy and attractive woman, who made it possible for Feuerbach to lead the simple, disciplined life of a private scholar. He stepped, "cleansed from a filthy bachelor existence, into the healthy bathwater of the holy state of matrimony," he claimed.

During this period, the staunch French skeptic Pierre Bayle (1647–1706), author of the best-selling four-volume *Historical and Critical Dictionary,* caught Feuerbach's attention. Although Bayle was not an atheist—he remained a member of the Reformed Church—Feuerbach called him a "hyperbolically caustic critic" and praised him for the way he analyzed the "conflict of God and world, heaven and earth, of grace and nature, spirit and flesh, reason and faith," discussed other religious problems, questioned the very existence of God, and suggested a society for committed atheists. Other important influences on Feuerbach included pantheists Benedict Spinoza and Jakob Böhme.

As a materialist, Feuerbach decided: "Philosophy is the science of reality in its truth and totality; but the embodiment of reality is nature. . . . Only a return to nature can bring us salvation."

Like Pascal, Feuerbach stressed will and heart, feeling and love, in addition to reason. Feuerbach's affections, however, were decidedly man-centered. He taught that God is nothing more than man's *projected* sense of his nature: "What man is not, but wills to be or wishes to be, just that and only that, nothing else, is God." In other words, Feuerbach argued that God didn't create man in his own image: instead, man projects his own best intentions and calls it "God."

Feuerbach claimed, "My atheism [is] merely the unconscious and actual atheism of modern humanity and science, made conscious, untwisted and openly declared."

Feuerbach saw materialistic atheism as "the secret of religion." He wasn't as interested in simply denying God. Instead, he advocated worshiping "God" for what he is—the real nature of man. His was no cold atheism but "anthropotheism." Feuerbach proposed that man wholeheartedly worship himself.

Feuerbach envisioned "a new age" in which "philosophy (as anthropology) becomes the new, true, atheistic 'religion.' " He saw his "political theology" as "the only practical and effective vehicle for politics," and definitely had revolution on his mind: "The purpose of my writings, as also of my lectures, is to turn men from theologians into anthropologists, from theophiles into philanthropists, from candidates for the hereafter into students of the here and now, from religious and political lackeys of the heavenly and earthly monarchy and aristocracy into free, self-confident citizens of the world."

Feuerbach's conception of anthropotheism captivated other revolutionary thinkers. Marx, Engels, and others found the reading of *The Essence of Christianity* to be their atheistic "revelatory experience" (although in a November 19, 1844, letter to Marx, Engels expressed second thoughts).

Feuerbach claimed he was living in a "period of the decline of Christianity" and declared, "Faith has been replaced by unbelief, the Bible by reason, religion and Church by politics, heaven by earth, prayer by work, hell by material wretchedness, the Christian by man."

In another place, the leading evangelist of materialistic atheism said his goal was to turn "friends of God into friends of man, believers into thinkers, worshipers into workers, candidates for the other world into students of this world, Christians, who on their own confession are half-animal and half-angel, into men—whole men."

Feuerbach succeeded in gaining a host of converts. No prominent form of atheism over the past one hundred and fifty years has failed to draw on his arguments:

- *Nothing exists simply because we want it to be.* God is simply man's projection of his best qualities, Feuerbach said. Yet, isn't man's nature flawed? If so, it is unworthy of worship. By dismissing God as God, Feuerbach has left no place for admitting the existence of evil, let alone dealing with guilt.
- *And, by inference, something doesn't exist if we don't want it to be.* God isn't relevant if you don't want him to be. Yet, who are we to say? What gives Feuerbach the right or authority to make such a claim? Is there no truth outside ourselves?

In the end, Feuerbach's arguments, though impressive, were flawed. Without scientific substantiation, he succeeded in obliterating the concept of a "rational" belief in God, an idea still felt today. His was a bold, relentless, thoroughgoing atheism to the bitter end.

And Feuerbach's end did prove bitter.

In the heady days of the 1848 revolution, when a comrade asked Feuerbach to take up arms, he replied: "I am now going to Heidelberg to lecture on the nature of religion to the students, and when in a hundred years' time a few grains grow up out of the seed I sow there, I shall have done more for the betterment of mankind than you with your blasting and bombarding."

Feuerbach's popularity rose and fell with that failed revolution.

After one term, he returned home from Heidelberg depressed, all too soon forgotten and isolated, and then bankrupt, utterly impoverished, dependent on charity, lethargic, and eventually weakened by a stroke.

Feuerbach lamented: "How the blasted dogs are barking again. My existence in Rechenberg is really a dog's life." Yet he refused to reconsider his atheism. After another stroke, Feuerbach lingered near death's door for quite some time, discarded, useless. He finally passed away at the age of sixty-eight and was buried in nearby Nuremberg.

Despite his personal failures, Feuerbach became the leading apostle of atheism, soon thereafter imitated by Marx and others.

THE FATHER OF COMMUNISM: MARX

The nineteenth-century German philosopher Karl Marx (1818–83) blasted away at many targets throughout his hard and difficult lifetime. Some of his fiercest attacks were aimed at the rich and powerful. Marx saw himself as the champion of the workingman, whom he envisioned leading to prosperity through his theories espousing the "imminent" downfall of capitalism and overthrow of the *haute bourgeoisie.*

As a follower of both Darwin and Feuerbach (about whom he wrote a book), Marx claimed: "Nowadays, in our evolutionary conception of the universe, there is absolutely no room for either a creator or a ruler." And, "Until now the philosophers have done nothing but interpret the world; now we have to transform it."

To effect that transformation, Marx took pen in hand and wielded it mightily. With Engels, Marx wrote *Theses on Feuerbach, Das Kapital,* and *The Communist Manifesto,* among other atheistic works.

Marx was born a Jew, raised a Christian, educated with ardent Catholics, and chose to become an atheist well before finishing his graduate studies.

He obtained his doctorate in 1841, at age twenty-three, for a dissertation titled, *The Difference between the Democritean and Epicurean Philosophy of Nature.* In the preface to that dissertation, he professed belief in atheism, quoting approvingly from *Prometheus Bound* and echoing Feuerbach's idea that "God" is merely man's projection of himself.

Yet only six years earlier, Marx had written a brilliant exposition of John 15:1–14, regarding the relationship of Jesus Christ to his disciples.

Marx turned from Christianity during his turbulent university days: after riotous living in his hometown, he transferred to the university in Berlin, where he embraced atheism, applauding Epicurus because he criticized "those who believe that man needs heaven."

Interestingly, Marx was an atheist for quite some time before he became a communist. In fact, his first real job was as editor-in-chief of a new periodical, in which Marx wrote *against* communism. It was only after moving to Paris, in 1843, under the influence of Engels and others, that Marx first became aware of economic issues (the growing workers' movement) and, under the influence of certain communists, joined their ranks.

In part because of his abrasiveness, Marx broke decisively with most of his early colleagues, blasting once close friends with his harsh, biting wit and philosophical powers. It was almost as if Marx couldn't define himself without attacking others, even his closest friends. Yet, strangely, he still admired at least some of those whom he attacked, including Hegel and later Feuerbach.

Once converted to communism, Marx applied to it his already strong atheistic convictions and articulated what became a united front for this growing revolutionary movement, already taking root in England, France, Germany, and Switzerland.

Marx saw atheism and communism as humanism's efforts to supersede the ideas of religion and private property. He saw no need to prove atheism, only apply it.

Most of Marx's writings were still incomplete when he died many years later; he left many unpublished fragments. His impulsiveness often meant that he took up a new cause long before completing the philosophical task at hand.

In one of his writings, Marx stated: "Religious distress is at the same time the expression of real distress and also the protest against real distress. Religion is the sigh of the oppressed creature, the heart of a heartless world, just as it is the spirit of spiritless conditions."

Yet Marx saw religion as too heavenly-minded to help humanity and—worse—a comfort from the sufferings of this present life. He decried religion as "the opiate of the people."

His goal? "To abolish religion as the illusory happiness of the people is to demand their real happiness. The demand to give up illusions about the existing state of affairs is the demand to give up a state of affairs which needs illusions. The criticism of religion is therefore in embryo the criticism of the vale of tears, the halo of which is religion."

Lenin later echoed Marx's sentiments: "Religion is opium for the people. Religion is a kind of spiritual intoxicant, in which the slaves of capital drown their humanity, and blunt their desire for a decent human existence."

According to Lenin, one of the objects of the Communist Party "is precisely to fight against all religious deception of the workers." He declared, "We must combat religion—this is the ABC of all materialism, and consequently Marxism."

It was only a short step from Lenin's hatred of religion to Josef Stalin's murderous persecutions of all peoples religious in a vain attempt to kill the idea of "God" across the vast former Soviet Union, Eastern Europe, and elsewhere.

Tens of millions died for Marx's cause.

THE FATHER OF NIHILISM: NIETZSCHE

Ten years after Feuerbach's death and a year before Marx passed away, fellow nineteenth-century German philosopher Friedrich Nietzsche (1844–1900) publicly proclaimed his *Requiem aeternam deo:* "God is dead. God remains dead. And we have killed him."

What a legacy. Nietzsche violently opposed Christianity, influenced the rise of fascism and Nazism in particular, and lent both myth and slogan to the past generation's short-lived but much-publicized enough-of-God movement.

During the turbulent 1960s, thousands of New Yorkers and tourists alike saw Nietzsche's slogan written in large, uneven capitals on the grimy wall of a subway at 116th Street and Broadway. Britisher Pauline Webb recalls the scene: " 'GOD IS DEAD,' it shouted, and in scrawled script underneath was added 'Signed by Nietzsche.' But someone had determined that that should not be the last word. By the side of the first slogan there was another: 'And now Nietzsche is dead—signed by God.' "

As a youth of only twenty, Nietzsche shocked his mother by refusing to take the sacrament at Easter services and told his sister Elizabeth that he had decided to pursue truth to the fullest, however "abhorrent or ugly" it might be. He decided such truth was nowhere to be found in Christianity: "No religion, directly or indirectly, either as dogma or as allegory, has ever contained a truth," Nietzsche later claimed.

Although an ardent fan of Strauss's *The Life of Jesus,* which had convinced Nietzsche to embrace atheism over against belief in God, he later severely blasted Strauss's "new faith" as nothing more than faith in science. Nietzsche claimed that Strauss had become little more than an apostle of Darwinism, utterly lacking the courage to take the next logical step and actively promote a new "morality" based on the survival of the fittest. According to Nietzsche, Strauss failed to understand that "the preaching of a morality is as easy as the establishment of it is difficult." Nietzsche prophesied that the end is coming for "virtually every morality that has hitherto been taught, reverenced and preached." He advocated the creation of a new breed of confident, courageous, conquering "supermen" (although he disbelieved in the notion of progress itself, evolutionary or otherwise).

Nietzsche also was greatly influenced by Schopenhauer, immediately embracing his philosophical pessimism upon reading *The World as Will and Idea.* In one of his writings, Nietzsche predicts: "Schopenhauer's question immediately comes to us in a terrifying way: Has existence any meaning at all? It will require a few centuries before this question can even be heard completely and in its full depth." Yet Nietzsche didn't completely buy into Schopenhauer's ideas; as time went on, Nietzsche admired more the *man* than his specific *message,* with which Nietzsche found several flaws.

Eventually, like Descartes, Nietzsche rejected everyone else's writings, complaining that even the most forthright atheists "lack passion in these things, they do not *suffer* from them." He also claimed, "One must have seen the fatality . . . one must have experienced it in oneself, one must have almost perished by it, no longer to find anything funny here." A humorist he was not.

Nietzsche advocated reversing all values, putting everything up for grabs, creating chaos of life as it is. He believed nihilism painted a huge question mark on everything in sight. Nietzsche admitted he was "a thoroughgoing nihilist," one who had lost faith in everything and everyone around him—in his fellow man and in civilization, culture, progress, modernity, morality, religion—all but himself.

In his last, autobiographical work—showing signs of strain that soon thereafter led to his breakdown—Nietzsche claimed: "I am no man, I am dynamite," "the first immoralist," "annihilator par excellence," "the first decent human being."

In his prime, Nietzsche remains unequaled in his fearlessness, in his ability to evoke mythic grandeur with his ideas, in his incredible sensory descriptions of abstract concepts, and in his remarkable predictions about future centuries.

On the opening page of the fifth part of his book, *The Gay Science,* for instance, Nietzsche quotes the terrible words of the Vicomte de Turenne, Marshal of France: "*Carcasse, tu trembles? Tu tremblerais bien davantage, si tu savais, où je te mène* [You tremble, carcass? You would tremble a lot more if you knew where I am taking you]." Nietzsche knew full well the awful implications of what he was writing: he used every means possible to convey their frightening reality to his readers.

In that same volume, Nietzsche tells his famous parable of the madman who rushes about proclaiming wildly, "God is dead." After reading the story even once, it's difficult to forget. The madman's message forcefully impresses itself on one's heart and mind. Why? In part, because of Nietzsche's effective use of deeply penetrating metaphorical questions to drive home his points.

In the story of the madman, Nietzsche compels us to consider the staggering implications of slaying God:

- "What after all are these churches now if they are not the tombs and sepulchers of God?"
- "Is not the greatness of this deed too great for us? Must we ourselves not become gods simply to appear worthy of it?"
- "How could we drink up the sea? Who gave us the sponge to wipe away the entire horizon? What were we doing when we unchained this earth from its sun? Whither is it moving now?"
- "Whither are we moving? Away from the sun? Are we not plunging continually? Backward, sideward, forward, in all directions?"
- "Is there still any up or down? Are we not straying as through an infinite nothing? Do we not feel the breath of empty space? Has it not become colder? Is not night continually closing in on us?"

Brrrrrrr. His very questions make us shudder, whether or not we buy into his grandiose ideas.

Furthermore, in writing about the God of Christianity "decomposing," Nietzsche evokes the senses and a torrent of emotions, speaking of a process that will take "thousands of years."

When Nietzsche declared, "God is dead," seven years before he went insane, he knew he was premature: the time for making such an announcement hadn't fully come yet. Nietzsche also correctly predicted that one of the consequences of this loss of religious faith in God would be a hundred years of nihilism: "Whence comes this uncanniest of all guests?" "Nihilism stands at the door." Almost prophetically, after years of insanity, Nietzsche died in the year 1900—and nihilism has indeed reigned with destructive fury throughout this past century.

In *The Antichrist,* written shortly before Nietzsche went insane in early 1889, he attacked nineteenth-century European Christianity's passivity and oppressive morality, railed against fourth-century Christianity's adverse effects on the Roman Empire, and lambasted its reversal of the "noble" values of the Greco-Roman world: "I call Christianity the one great curse, the one enormous and innermost perversion, the one great instinct of revenge, for which no means are too venomous, too underhand, too underground, and too petty." Nietzsche spared no one except Jesus, saying the only Christian worthy of the name had died on a Roman cross.

In several earlier works, Nietzsche did quote and speak approvingly of Pascal, who (like Hegel) had used the idea of the "death of God" (a religious phrase previously used only of Christ's death on the cross) to deplore the growing sense of Christian *un*belief in Europe.

Nietzsche chastised his generation for having "never gone through a seventeenth century of hard self-examination, like the French" and said, "Pascal I almost love, for he has given me infinite instruction; he is the only *logical* Christian." Yet, after reading Strauss and Schopenhauer, Nietzsche rejected Pascal's Wager (described in Chapter 8): On this one point, Nietzsche decided, Pascal was wrong—and the "death of God" took on yet another new meaning.

As a man "born before his time," Nietzsche may rightly be considered the twentieth century's first philosopher. His dogma profoundly and tragically influenced the careers of Hitler, Stalin, and Mussolini, who bear direct responsibility for sending tens of millions of men, women, youths, and children to their deaths.

Nietzsche's writings also had a great influence on Bernard Shaw, D. H. Lawrence, W. B. Yeats, and other important writers, as well as on Sigmund Freud, Carl Gustav Jung, and other leading psychoanalysts. Freud went so far as to claim that Nietzsche achieved a level of personal psychoanalytic insight unequaled by anyone else in history (before going insane, of course).

One cannot understand the insanity of the past century without understanding Nietzsche's role in shaping it. Where Feuerbach and Marx and others feared to tread, Nietzsche boldly led the way: exploring the full implications of all-out atheism.

THE FATHER OF PSYCHOANALYSIS: FREUD

Early in his career, influenced by the writings of Darwin and others, the Austrian physician Sigmund Freud (1856–1939) turned from aiding the healing of the body to attempting to heal the soul. By founding psychoanalysis, Freud sought to venture further into the human psyche than anyone had previously attempted.

Today, many people almost take for granted Freud's insights about the nature of neurosis, recognizing the unconscious, seeking to understand dreams, and probing what we've previously repressed.

As a convinced atheist, Freud believed religion was a "universal obsessional neurosis," so universal that he felt compelled to understand why, if God is a myth, religion is so prevalent in human experience.

In his book, *The Future of an Illusion,* Freud claimed that the Judeo-Christian faith, in particular, is an illusion created by our feelings of impotence to control ourselves, let alone nature. To make sense of the world and bring a measure of comfort to our souls, Freud said, we've accepted the infantile illusion of a divine father figure. In its essence, therefore, religion is devoid of truth.

Although he had to admit that religion is "perhaps the most important item in the psychical inventory of a civilization," Freud called it a collective neurosis, thoroughly renounced it, and advocated that his followers venture into "hostile life and strive for a new religion through science."

Why such antagonism toward traditional religion?

In part, Freud overestimated the works of Darwin, Strauss, Feuerbach, Nietzsche, and others, which he felt had thoroughly undermined the credibility of religion.

Freud's rage against all things religious, however, went deeper than that.

Freud was born in Moravia and grew up in Vienna, the son of a Jewish wool merchant who had been educated as an Orthodox Jew yet had become liberal in his attitudes toward Jewish tradition. According to Ernest Jones, Freud's student and biographer, "Freud himself was certainly conversant with all Jewish customs and festivals," if not the details of Jewish theology, as such.

Yet Freud rejected the Jewish faith (and Christianity) after many bitter experiences with anti-Semitism during his youth. In one instance, Freud's father was publicly humiliated by an obnoxious "Christian" lad. Instead of rebuking the boy, the senior Freud swallowed the insult, pulled his new fur cap out of the mud, and proceeded home. In one stroke, Sigmund lost respect for his father.

At the University of Vienna, Freud felt the bitter sting of anti-Semitism himself. Recalling those days fifty years later, Freud remembered: "Above all, I found that I was expected to feel myself inferior and an alien because I was a Jew. I refused absolutely to do the first of these things."

During his university days, Freud became a staunch atheist. It wasn't until years later that he pioneered his first psychoanalytic theories. The chronology is important to note: Freud himself made it clear that psychoanalysis doesn't presuppose or necessarily lead to atheism.

Still, Freud used his growing influence in the early decades of the twentieth century to advocate atheism, drawing on the arguments of Feuerbach and others who had gone before him: "All I have done—and this is the only thing that is new in my exposition—is to add some psychological foundation to the criticisms of my great predecessors."

From Feuerbach, Freud understood theological concepts as projections of man's greatest aspirations, illusions (delusions) without any demonstrable basis in reality. "Religious ideas are fulfillments of the oldest, strongest and most urgent wishes of mankind," Freud said. Any thoughts of heaven, hell, or other concepts of the hereafter, therefore, are mere "psychomythology."

Jack Miles won a Pulitzer Prize in 1996 for *God: A Biography.* The *New York Times Book Review* describes his book this way: "The Judeo-Christian Supreme Being is not only a spiritual construct but a literary creation, studied here in the context of the Tanakh, the Hebrew Bible. The author, a former Jesuit, finds God to be a player of many roles in His own story, and quite ambivalent about His chief creation."

Who created whom?

And who's ambivalent about whom?

Miles merely repeats (albeit eloquently) what many have been saying for a long time: that God is nothing more than a figment of humanity's imagination. Freud would have wholeheartedly agreed.

Freud claimed: "We shall tell ourselves that it would be very nice if there were a moral order in the universe and an after-life; but it is a very striking fact that all this is exactly as we are bound to wish it to be. And it would be more remarkable still if our wretched, ignorant and downtrodden ancestors had succeeded in solving all these difficult riddles of the universe."

Like many of his contemporaries, Freud saw contemporary Western civilization as vastly superior to other people's in other times, mostly thanks to a rapid series of "scientific" advances that have eliminated any need for religious "superstitions."

Of his faith in science, Freud said: "If this belief is an illusion, then we are in the same position as you [believers]. But science has given us evidence by its numerous and important successes that it is no illusion." And, "No, our science is no illusion. But an illusion it would be to suppose that what science cannot give us we can get elsewhere."

It's telling that some of Freud's own "scientific" theories fell on hard times, including his detailed descriptions of the scope and meaning of totem worship in primitive cultures, which further research soon proved wrong at almost every turn.

Yet Freud's theories eventually became culturally fashionable and were essentially swallowed whole by many Western intellectuals within twenty years of the publication of his first major work, *The Interpretation of Dreams,* which came out the same year Nietzsche died.

In that particular volume, Freud laid the foundation for many of his latter works by arguing that "Dreams are wish fulfillments." He regarded that book as one of his two most important even though, six years after its publication, it had sold a mere three hundred fifty-one copies and only three people had attended his first series of lectures on the subject.

Persistence pays when you're advocating new ideas.

Yet, like a Polaroid picture in reverse, most new ideas fade after a while. The test of time is the most telling of all.

Küng rightly observes: "Neither the 'nullification of religion' by atheistic humanism (Feuerbach) nor the 'withering away of religion' to be brought about by atheistic socialism (Marx) nor the 'supersession of religion' by atheistic science (Freud) has proved to be a true prognosis."

The triumphal declarations of the leading apostles of atheism—especially Nietzsche—reached their pinnacle of influence by the 1960s, when *Time* magazine asked, "Is God Dead?"

Yet only a decade later, *Time* wondered, "Is Marx Dead?"

And two decades after that, "Is Freud Dead?"

At least, not his ideas. Not yet.

@#&*! SAYS IT ALL?

Speaking to university students on their turf is always a bit unnerving, but when communist radicals try to shout you down, you quickly begin to think about canceling your upcoming lectures at other universities.

At the University of Sydney, I was speaking to eight hundred students on the mall about what Jesus Christ can do for a nation when a group of Marxist-Leninists began shouting obscenities at me.

I kept going, mentioning former U.S. Secretary of State Henry Kissinger's observation during the cold war that there were no more than twenty-four free nations left in the world. One striking characteristic of those twenty-four nations: all had been profoundly influenced by Christian awakenings within the past two or three centuries. I then reminded the students that they were reaping the benefits of living in a nation that had been blessed because of its Christian roots.

Even if a nation was now thoroughly secular and in need of massive change, "there is only one revolution that works," I told the students, "and that's the revolution in the heart through faith in Jesus Christ."

Those remarks prompted one Marxist agitator (who looked rather like Fidel Castro in his younger days) to point his finger at me and shout gross obscenities. I tried to engage him in an intelligent debate, but all he knew were swear words, readily suggesting he had no basis for his doctrine.

The basis for the Christian faith, meanwhile, is rock-solid, despite the most bitter and profane attempts of godless individuals to destroy it. Instead, atheism itself is thoroughly discredited.

Chapter 11

REASONS TO DISBELIEVE?

Many people will do almost anything to escape pain or get their own way.

Noted psychologist William Glasser wrote that "suffering always drives us to try unrealistic means to fulfill our needs."

In a state of heightened self-awareness and acute pain, the apostles of atheism cursed their fate, spat on the organized Church, rejected Judeo-Christian morality, and asserted their independence "without hope and without God in this world" (Ephesians 2:12).

Yet did they have sufficient cause for such actions? Or were they using unrealistic means to satisfy deeply felt needs?

I'm convinced that even the most well articulated reasons to disbelieve God are spiritually and morally bankrupt, devoid of truth, removed from reality.

REASON NO. 1: THE PROBLEM OF EVIL AND SUFFERING

When asked what questions they would like to ask God if given the opportunity, forty-four percent of Americans said they want to know, "Why is there evil or suffering in the world?"

John Hick noted, "To many, the most powerful positive objection to belief in God is the fact of evil." Peter Kreeft agrees, saying, "The strongest argument for atheism has always been the problem of evil." That's been the case the past twenty-five hundred years, since the days of Buddha's "enlightenment."

True, evil and suffering plague us all. Is that any reason to disavow God?

The ancient Greek philosopher Epicurus (342?–270 B.C.) stated the problem in four parts: "God either wishes to take away evil, and is unable, or He is able, and unwilling; or He is neither willing nor able, or He is both willing and able. If He is willing and is unable, He is feeble, which is not in accordance with the character of God; if He is able and unwilling, He is envious, which is equally at variance with God; if He is neither willing nor able, He is both envious and feeble, and therefore not God: if He is both willing and able, which alone is suitable to God, from what source then are evils? or why does He not remove them?"

What Epicurus failed to consider is that, in light of his eternal purposes, God may choose to allow evil for a time. It wasn't his idea, it's certainly not his ideal, but he's not going to instantly obliterate the universe to eradicate it, either.

Still, many atheists cite this problem as proof positive that they know better than God. Nietzsche, for one, called God "the greatest immoralist in deeds that has ever existed" and decried religious theories that attempt to explain human suffering as equally immoral, especially those theories that infer that suffering is rightly brought on as a divine punishment of humanity's supposed sinfulness.

Some writers claim the problem of evil and suffering actually is the source of humanity's varied religious impulses. Echoing Feuerbach, Holbach, and Freud all in one breath, atheist Michael J. Buckley remarked recently that the aboriginal source of religion "is ignorance and terror, and the model on which the imagination fashions its creations is the human person writ large. Once fashioned, this chimerical agent is open to prayers and sacrifices, appeal of penitence and self-denial, which will disarm his anger and control the outrages of nature. Religion is the magical way of controlling the causes of human tragedy."

The implication? Buckley is blunt: atheism evolves into antitheism, actively seeking to destroy religion, which he sees as opposed to his "scientific" way of thinking.

"Take, for example, the attribute of 'goodness,' " writes Buckley. "Theologians call god 'good,' and human beings have some idea what is contained in that predicate. Then realize that this god is also omnipotent. Try to combine these two predicates in the face of human pain, the desolation of war, the destruction of earthquakes and disease. It makes no sense to say that this omnipotent god is good. . . . The goodness of an omnipotent god is contradicted at every turn of human history."

Buckley claims it makes more sense to say this life doesn't make any sense at all; nature alone calls the shots, arbitrarily, certainly without any reference to morality, necessity, or purpose.

Hans Küng observes that "even in antiquity, philosophers strove in the name of morality to deprive the gods of power, a tradition that can be traced up to Nietzsche, Sartre and Camus."

Albert Camus, the French writer and philosopher, rejected God for allowing the world to be a place "in which children suffer and die." His answer, then? Indiscriminate rebellion—as if that could possibly make things better.

What about classic Christianity? Philosopher Mortimer Adler says: "Christianity is the only logical, consistent faith in the world. But there are elements to it that can only be described as mystery."

In writing about the origin of evil, John H. Gerstner admitted: "This is the most difficult problem in all of theistic theology and philosophy." Yet to be honest to reality, we must consistently avoid the irrational options of denying the existence of evil or of God.

If any period of history has conclusively proved the reality of evil, it's the twentieth century. Fifty years ago, Albert Einstein said it bluntly: "I do not fear the explosive power of the atom bomb. What I fear is the explosive power of evil in the human heart."

Thomas E. Dewey stated: "Our problem is within ourselves. We have found the means to blow the world physically apart. Spiritually, we have yet to find the means to put together the world's broken pieces."

More recently, Arthur C. Clark lamented, "This is the first age that has paid any attention to the future; which is a little ironic seeing that we may not have one."

In the face of such actual and potential evil, does religion offer any hope?

Actor Richard Gere says he was disappointed by what he found in Christianity: "I was raised a Methodist but found that Christian religions failed to answer crucial questions like, What is the nature of suffering and where does suffering come from? How can suffering exist? Why does evil exist? Why did God create good and evil? I finally found [in Buddhism] a system willing to engage those questions and many more."

For Gere, as a Buddhist, suffering is the result of an evil act and bad karma. What he missed back in Sunday school, had he read his Bible, is that Christianity takes the issue of suffering very seriously. Only four chapters in all the Bible—the first two in Genesis and the last two in the book of Revelation—say nothing about sin's terrible consequences.

The scope of this book doesn't allow me to address Gere's questions at length. Others already have covered this subject well. In his book, *The Problem of Pain,* for instance, C. S. Lewis wrote: "God whispers to us in our pleasures, speaks in our conscience, but shouts in our pains: it is His megaphone to rouse a deaf world."

In *A Severe Mercy,* Sheldon Vanauken in turn asked God some tough questions when his young wife died: "How could things go on when the world had come to an end? How could things—how could I—go on in this void? How could one person, not very big, leave an emptiness that was galaxy-wide?"

Still, let's briefly consider the crucial questions Gere raises.

What is the nature of suffering? The Bible says both humanity and nature suffer the consequences of humanity's sins against God and of hurtful deeds against one another. We both sin and are sinned against.

Novelist Harriet K. Feder suggests that, in times of great evil and suffering, the question we should ask is not "Where is God?" but "Where is man?"

Stanley Hauerwas, professor of ethics at Duke University, says that, when a disabled child is born, the religious question we should ask is not "Why does God permit mental retardation in His world?" but "What sort of community should we become so that mental retardation need not be a barrier to a child's enjoying a gratifying life?"

Dr. Harold O. J. Brown, director of the Rockford Institute Center on Religion and Society, observes that "an unfocused, intuitive awareness of God, without knowing Him personally, leaves us totally bewildered by and unprepared for the suffering of this world."

Much suffering is the result of sin, whether our own transgressions or the iniquities of others. Brown says: "The scope of human sin from Adam to the present, the pain it caused and continues to cause, is an incredible burden. As the Lutheran theologian Paul Althaus expressed it, the burden would be too much to bear except for two world-transforming facts: first, the victory Christ won on the cross over Satan and sin; second, His impending return in glory."

Brown continues: "These truths do not solve the problem of evil or answer all of the questions it forces on us here in time, but they do put everything in perspective. Philosophers and theologians can help us deal with the problem of evil, but the ultimate answer will come only when 'God will wipe away every tear from [our] eyes' (Revelation 7:17)."

Where does suffering come from? The Bible gives four specific answers.

First, from natural disasters, such as an earthquake or a storm. The suffering that results from these disasters happens to both the righteous and the unrighteous (Matthew 5:45).

Second, from man's inhumanity to man, including armed conflicts. Because of greed and pride, individuals try to hurt others (James 4:1–2).

Third, from our own erroneous actions. If I walk off the roof of my office and fall to the ground, breaking my leg, I am suffering because I broke God's laws of physics. We also suffer when we break God's moral laws. Some, not all, suffering is allowed by God as a punishment for sin. Often, God simply lets us live with the consequences of our actions (Galatians 6:7–8).

Fourth, from the unseen hand of Satan, our adversary. The abiding lesson of the book of Job, one of the oldest Hebrew Scriptures, is that even the wisest of men and women cannot always comprehend in a purely rational manner where evil, suffering, and pain come from. Often it can be understood only from a divine perspective, from the propositional revelation that God is far above us, God is good, God is in control (even though Satan opposes us), God has his purposes, and God will gain the victory through our perseverance.

The one mistake we dare not make, Philip Yancey reminds us, is to confuse *God* (who is good) with *life* (which is hard). God feels the same way we do—and is taking the most radical steps possible (Christmas, Good Friday, Easter, and more to come) to redeem the present situation.

How can suffering exist? In a remarkable exercise of his sovereignty, God has given humanity the freedom to make moral choices. In more than twenty passages, the Bible clearly states that every person makes wrong moral choices. Because by nature we tend to choose our will over and against God's will, "all have sinned and fallen short of the glory of God" (Romans 3:23). Such acts of rebellion against God produce most heartaches and suffering.

An atheist may rightly reject such an answer, but only if he or she is first willing to face a much more difficult question. Harold Kushner describes the atheist's dilemma this way: "He has to explain why there is love, honesty, generosity, courage, and altruism in the world, and why it feels so good and so right when we let those qualities into our lives."

Scott Peck concurs: "Dozens of times I have been asked by patients or acquaintances: 'Dr. Peck, why is there evil in the world?' Yet no one has ever asked me in all these years: 'Why is there good in the world?' It is as if we automatically assume this is a naturally good world that has somehow been contaminated by evil. . . . The mystery of goodness is even greater than the mystery of evil." Whether due to a brain tumor or debilitating syndrome, no one ever has uncontrolled fits of goodness.

Still, *Why does evil exist?* Contrary to Gere's thinking, the Bible makes it clear that God did not create evil. Evil entered the universe through the fall of Satan, an archangel who dared to rival the Almighty.

The prophet Isaiah gives us a picture of this: "You said in your heart, 'I will ascend to heaven; I will raise my throne above the stars of God; I will sit enthroned on the mount of assembly, on the utmost heights of the sacred mountain. I will ascend above the tops of the clouds; I will make myself like the Most High.' But you are brought down to the grave, to the depths of the pit" (Isaiah 14:13–15).

Another prophet writes: " 'You were blameless in your ways from the day you were created till wickedness was found in you. . . . So I drove you in disgrace from the mount of God, and I expelled you, O guardian cherub, from among the fiery stones. Your heart became proud on account of your beauty, and you corrupted your wisdom because of your splendor. So I threw you to the earth; I made a spectacle of you before kings' " (Ezekiel 28:15–17).

Jesus himself said, "I saw Satan fall like lightning from heaven" (Luke 10:18).

But before his expulsion from heaven, Satan drew perhaps a third of the angels into his rebellion. Ever since, the Devil has schemed against God and his people. Satan knows he's doomed but, like any common criminal, he wants to take as many with him as he can. Misery loves company, but the tragic irony is that hell will be the epitome of loneliness.

Some joke that they want to spend eternity in hell so they can party with their friends. Yet hell, by definition, is separation from relationship with God and others forever. In the words of C. S. Lewis, "The only place outside Heaven where you can be perfectly safe from all the dangers and perturbations of love is Hell."

No wonder Jesus warned, "Do not be afraid of those who kill the body but cannot kill the soul. Rather, be afraid of the one who can destroy both soul and body in hell" (Matthew 10:28).

So, while the problem of evil and suffering *is* serious, it certainly isn't sufficient cause for unbelief or rebellion against God. Instead, it should drive us to God, humbly asking for his will to "be done on earth as it is in heaven" (Matthew 6:10).

REASON NO. 2: THE REJECTION OF (BAD) RELIGION

The sins of the Church may have incited more rebellion against God than anything else.

It doesn't make sense. Ernest Nagel declared: "Atheism has been, in effect, a moral revulsion against the undoubted abuses of the secular power exercised by religious leaders and religious institutions," especially in countries with strong state churches.

Examples of those "undoubted abuses"? Nagel claimed that over the past few centuries, in various situations, "Religious authorities have opposed the correction of glaring injustices, and encouraged politically and socially reactionary policies. Religious institutions have been havens of obscurantist thought and centers for the dissemination of intolerance. Religious creeds have been used to set limits to free inquiry, to perpetuate inhumane treatment of the ill and the underprivileged, and to support moral doctrines insensitive to human suffering."

Nagel admitted, "These indictments may not tell the whole story about the historical significance of religion; but they are at least an important part of the story."

His conclusion? "The refutation of theism has thus seemed to many as an indispensable step not only towards liberating men's minds from superstition, but also towards achieving a more equitable reordering of society."

While Nagel's dreams of the "reordering of society" have not reached fruition in America, his motivations for wanting to pursue that goal are telling.

Aldous Huxley said: "Belief in a personal God has released an enormous amount of energy directed towards good ends; but it has probably released an equal amount of energy directed towards ends that were silly, or mad, or downright evil."

Bertrand Russell claimed: "Religion is based . . . primarily and mainly upon fear . . . fear of the mysterious, fear of defeat, fear of death. Fear is the parent of cruelty, and therefore it is no wonder if cruelty and religion have gone hand in hand." He regarded religion "as a disease born of fear and as a source of untold misery to the human race."

Paul Edwards advocated the elimination of religious belief: "I am totally convinced . . . that all the metaphysical claims of traditional religions are untenable; and I am equally convinced that, although here and there religious institutions may have done some good, for the most part they have caused and continue to cause a great deal of harm and mischief."

Edwards admitted that the loss of religious belief and "authoritarian and repressive morality associated with it" would cause distress and confusion, but claimed it would, in the long run, benefit the human race.

For most of the past four centuries, rejection of *God* has been rejection of the *Church* at its worst. In North America, theologians J. I. Packer and Thomas Howard admit that "the enforcing of substandard Christianity in homes, churches, schools, and communities has inflicted so much emotional hurt, that anti-Christian reaction is now marked by a strong head of emotional steam."

Packer and Howard describe various agnostic and atheistic movements and conclude that "a single conviction animates them all—namely, the belief that current cultural developments, especially those which claim the name of science, show religion to be irrational and hostile to human happiness. The thought is that only those who know they are on their own in the universe, with no God to worship and no concern about the church, will ever take the bold steps that are needed to set their lives straight."

They go on to say these secular, humanistic movements are a "reaction born, as it seems, of hurt and resentment, outrage and disgust at the tenets and track record of organized religion. In this the humanist spirit is older than Christianity."

Furthermore, "It is clear that many humanists in the West are stirred by a sense of outrage at what professed Christians, past and present, have done; and this makes them see their humanism as a kind of crusade, with the killing of Christianity as its prime goal."

Why such anti-God crusades? Packer and Howard write: "It was observation and experience of the bad Christianity of a church (Roman Catholic, allied to a corrupt power structure) that produced the anti-Christian hostility of the French Revolution. It was observation of the bad Christianity of churches (Protestant: the Prussian state church, and later the Church of England, both of which were stagnant and aloof from working people) which convinced Marx that religion is the opiate of the masses, needing to be abolished; and it was a similar experience of bad Christianity in the Russian Orthodox Church that set the leaders of the Russian revolution to work carrying out Marx's program."

Packer and Howard themselves write against "bad Christianity—Christianity that lacks honesty, or intelligence, or regard for truth, or biblical depth, or courtesy, or all of these together."

Many other Christian writers have decried the sins of the Church, as well, including Dorothy Sayers, who called them God's third great humiliation, after the incarnation (Christmas) and the cross (Good Friday).

Has the Church always been this bad?

Centuries after the horrific crusades and inquisitions and other "holy" wars, Muslims, Jews, Catholics, and Protestants still are fighting selected "holy wars."

Yet Peck writes: "Crusades and inquisitions have nothing to do with Christ. War, torture, and persecution have nothing to do with Christ. Arrogance and revenge have nothing to do with Christ. When he gave his one recorded sermon, the first words out of Jesus' mouth were, 'Blessed are the poor in spirit.' Not the arrogant. And as he was dying he asked that his murderers be forgiven."

Jesus Christ should not be rejected for the sins of humanity, but instead embraced as Savior and Lord. Religion isn't the answer to our problems, obviously. Relationship with God through Christ is. Will you put your trust in him?

Noted British statesman William Wilberforce put it well: "Just as we would not discard liberty because people abuse it, nor patriotism, nor courage, nor reason, speech, and memory—though all abused—no more should we eliminate true religion because self-seekers have perverted it."

Motivated by the love of Jesus Christ, Christians have done enormous good, as even Nagel, Huxley, and Edwards had to admit. Consider what true Christianity has contributed to the welfare of all humanity:

- The Bible, "the Book of books," wholly or partially translated and published in more than 2,140 languages. E. D. Hirsch, Jr., author of *Cultural Literacy* and many other works, describes the Bible as must reading for literate youth and adults, saying, "The linguistic and cultural importance of the Bible is a fact that no one denies."

- A wealth of other great literature, including the works of Augustine, John Calvin, Dante Alighieri, John Bunyan, Feodor Dostoevsky, Leo Tolstoy, Blaise Pascal, Aleksandr Solzhenitsyn, Martin Luther, Jonathan Edwards, Charles Dickens, John Milton, Daniel Defoe, Alfred Lord Tennyson, Hans Christian Andersen, J. R. R. Tolkien, Dorothy Sayers, Flannery O'Connor, and C. S. Lewis.
- Linguistic and literacy work among more than 1,210 people groups worldwide, making it possible for countless tens of millions of people to read the Bible and other literature in their own language.
- World-famous musical compositions by Johann Sebastian Bach, George Frederic Handel, Felix Mendelssohn, Wolfgang Amadeus Mozart, and many others.
- Great works of art by Leonardo da Vinci, Michelangelo, Raphael, Rembrandt, et al.
- Many of the ideals embodied in the Bill of Rights and Constitution of the United States of America, including the value of life, the priority of liberty, the existence of inalienable rights endowed by our Creator, and the necessity of establishing justice. Presidents Washington, Lincoln, Grant, Garfield, McKinley, Wilson, Franklin D. Roosevelt, Eisenhower, Reagan, Bush, and Clinton, among others, have publicly reaffirmed aspects of America's Christian heritage.
- A blueprint for strong, healthy marriages and families—sacred institutions which form the backbone of any civilization—and a new standard recognizing the dignity of women and children, unlike anything previously seen in the Greco-Roman world. This is seen both in the ministry of Jesus and his first-century disciples, who were subsequently accused by their persecutors in at least one Roman city of "turning the world upside down."
- The moral courage to abolish such human rights abuses as infanticide and gladiatorial combat within the Roman Empire, slavery and child labor in the British Empire, and cannibalism among various primitive (animist) groups of people.
- The charity to help any and all in need through the establishment of thousands of medical hospitals, emergency shelters for

individuals and families displaced from their homes, homes for orphans and others in need, humanitarian institutions for the mentally insane, ministries to the victims of crimes, and chaplaincy ministries to service personnel, prisoners, hospital patients and their families.

- The wisdom to promote education for all by the establishment of tens of thousands of schools, colleges, seminaries, and universities throughout America and around the world.
- The insight to advocate the prevention of cruelty against animals (almost unknown outside Christianized cultures) and careful stewardship of the environment, in light of humanity's God-given mandate after creation.

While secular forces have adopted many of these causes over the years, the fact is Christians often have been at the forefront, advancing the good and positive aspects of Western Christian civilization over the past two millennia.

Several historians, including J. Wesley Bready, Keith J. Hardman, Kenneth Scott Latourette, Philip Schaff, and Ruth A. Tucker, have suggested that the example and teachings of Jesus Christ have had far more effect, for good, than those of any other individual in history. I concur wholeheartedly.

While the spirit of the Church may be noble, and its good deeds exemplary, the vices perpetrated in its name still remain a huge stumbling block for many. I challenge you to look beyond the failings of supposedly religious persons directly to Jesus Christ:

"Let us fix our eyes on Jesus, the author and perfecter of our faith, who for the joy set before him endured the cross, scorning its shame, and sat down at the right hand of the throne of God. Consider him who endured such opposition from sinful men, so that you will not grow weary and lose heart" (Hebrews 12:2–3).

Isn't it personal sinfulness, after all, that causes most individuals to rebel against God and his purposes?

REASON NO. 3: THE DESIRE FOR MORAL LICENSE

Paul Little noted that the most compelling arguments against God and the Church are "often smokescreens for moral rebellion."

Harold Kushner observes that, when Dostoevsky wrote the line, "If there is no God, everything is permitted," he meant more than "I can do whatever I want." Kushner says, "I suspect he means 'Without God, what makes something I do wrong? It may be illegal. It may be distasteful to you. It may hurt people who don't deserve to be hurt. But if I feel good doing it, what makes it *wrong?*' "

Indeed, without a divine point of reference, who's to say what's right and wrong?

Let's explore the specific personal and broader social ramifications of this question briefly.

Gerstner argued that "men often corrupt their thinking by their prejudices and seek to justify their errors for some ulterior motive. Frequently they are even unwilling to listen to a divergent view because they refuse to entertain its unacceptable implications."

We see this in Nietzsche's vicious rejection of the "slave morality" of Christianity in favor of what he called the "master morality" of nihilism, which permitted him, among other things, to relentlessly lust after a friend's wife to the day he went insane. And we see it in the illicit sexual affairs of Hegel, Feuerbach, Schopenhauer, Marx, Nietzsche, Freud, Sartre, Bertrand Russell, and even Albert Einstein, that great icon of relativity who refused to accept classic Judeo-Christian doctrine and ethics.

Russell called Christianity "the principal enemy of moral progress [including sexual liberation] in the world."

In *Ends and Means,* atheistic revolutionary Aldous Huxley admitted: "I had motives for not wanting the world to have a meaning; consequently I assumed that it had none, and was able without any difficulty to find satisfying reasons for this assumption. Most ignorance is vincible ignorance. We don't know because we don't want to know."

And what were those motives? Huxley wrote: "For myself as, no doubt, for most of my contemporaries, the philosophy of meaninglessness was essentially an instrument of liberation. The liberation we desired was simultaneously liberation from a certain political and economic system and liberation from a certain system of morality. We objected to the morality because it interfered with our sexual freedom."

He went on to say: "The supporters of these systems claimed that in some way they embodied the meaning (a Christian meaning, they insisted) of the world. There was one admirably simple method of confuting these people and at the same time justifying ourselves in our political and erotic revolt: We could deny that the world had any meaning whatsoever."

This philosophy of meaninglessness is exactly what George Orwell warned about in *1984*: our society is buying into the idea that words can be twisted for moral and political ends. Among other places, this is evident in academia.

According to the *Wall Street Journal,* "The campus culture wars may be entering a new phase, and this time the good guys finally seem to be pulling ahead."

Exhibit A?

A young New York University physicist, Alan Sokal, submitted an essay titled, "Transgressing the Boundaries: Toward a Transformative Hermeneutics of Quantum Gravity," to *Social Text,* a trendy left-wing quarterly edited at NYU and published by Duke University Press. The essay was "deliberate nonsense from start to finish."

Sokal submitted the essay to see whether "a leading North American journal of cultural studies . . . would publish an article liberally salted with nonsense if (a) it sounded good and (b) it flattered the editors' ideological preconceptions."

The answer?

Yes.

As soon as his essay appeared, Sokal revealed the hoax in *Lingua Franca.* "The story clearly struck a nerve," the *Wall Street Journal* reported, especially because Sokal himself identifies himself as a "leftist" too. Other periodicals and network television news shows quickly picked up the story, leaving the editors of *Social Text* furious.

The question many asked, of course, is, Why did *Social Text* publish Sokal's bogus essay in the first place? "The short answer is that they were unable to recognize that it was a joke," Roger Kimball writes in the *Wall Street Journal.* "Nor was this surprising. For, although 'Transgressing the Boundaries' is nonsensical, it is no more nonsensical than most of the other pieces in that issue of *Social Text.*"

If the advocates of cultural studies are right that truth is a "social construction," Sokal observed in *Lingua Franca,* then the result is that "incomprehensibility becomes a virtue; allusions, metaphors and puns substitute for evidence and logic."

Stanley Fish, the infamous Duke deconstructionist who is also executive director of the Duke University Press, wrote a long Op-Ed piece, published in the *New York Times,* attacking Sokal for perpetrating this hoax.

Kimball states: "He [Fish] began by assuring his readers that cultural studies really pose no threat to the scientific notion of truth. . . . He also charged that it was really Mr. Sokal, not the advocates of cultural studies, who threatened to 'undermine . . . intellectual studies.' But then Mr. Fish is the man who once wrote that 'there is no such thing as literal meaning' and then went on to tell his readers not to worry because truth didn't really matter.

"Of course, it does matter. And the controversy sparked by Alan Sokal's hoax may finally convince college deans and presidents, parents and alumni, legislators and trustees, to take a hard look at the politicized nonsense they have been conned into subsidizing."

Kimball calls such nonsense a "new form of academic barbarism," whereby beliefs are shaped by one's politics—not truth. In this case, the politics of *Social Text* are decidedly Marxist—and it shows.

When Charles Darwin was asked whether man was in any way unique from other life forms, he replied: "Man is the only animal that blushes." Mark Twain later quipped, "Sure, man is the only animal with good reason to blush." No matter how hard we try to reject standards of right and wrong, we all have them. Even if they're skewed and sometimes don't make sense.

Media giant and self-described agnostic Ted Turner once remarked, rather sternly, that the "people of this age shouldn't be told to do anything."

Shouldn't?

Unless we have a basis on which to say what's right and wrong, it doesn't work to try to make value statements. Yet some basis is essential.

Atheist J. L. Mackie suggested: "Moral properties constitute so odd a cluster of qualities and relations that they are most unlikely to have arisen in the ordinary course of events without an all-powerful god to create them."

Fellow atheist Kai Nielsen goes three steps further: "It is the claim of many influential Jewish and Christian theologians (Brunner, Buber, Barth, Niebuhr and Bultmann—to take outstanding examples) that the only genuine basis for morality is in religion. And any old religion is not good enough. The only truly adequate foundation for moral belief is a religion that acknowledges that absolute sovereignty of the Lord, found in the prophetic religions."

Nielsen adds: "The sense of moral relativism, skepticism and nihilism rampant in our age is due in large measure to the general weakening of religious belief in an age of science. Without God there can be no objective foundation for our moral beliefs. . . . Without religious belief, without the Living God, there could be no adequate answer to the persistently gnawing questions: What ought we to do? How ought I to live?"

Still, Nielsen is quick to point out: "These theologians will readily grant what is plainly true, namely, that as a matter of fact many nonreligious people behave morally, but they contend that without a belief in God and his law there is no ground or reason for being moral."

Ravi Zacharias says: "Any antitheist who lives a moral life merely lives *better* than his or her philosophy warrants."

Packer and Howard state that the attempts of various secular movements "to devise a way of life more humane than its Christian counterpart actually produces one which is less so: less compassionate, less free, less hopeful, less dignified, less respectful, less patient; one that is more bleak, harsh, savage, gloomy, and—let us face it—dull altogether."

Nevertheless, "We do not deny that . . . there are many [atheistic] humanists whose conscientious goodness puts Christians to shame, humanists who are in fact much better than their creed."

Rabbi Harold Kushner writes: "I have to admit that some of my best friends are atheists. They never darken the doorway of either church or synagogue," yet are good people, while some regular synagogue members are "small-souled people, insecure and judgmental, quick to find fault with others."

Atheism has amassed a horrific track record, however, over the past century. Charles Pierre Baudelaire saw a bright side to such tragedies: "Man's vices, horrible as they are supposed to be, contain the positive proof of his taste for the infinite."

Yet more than a taste is required. Glasser reminds us: "All society is based on morality." In *Tractatus Logico-philosophicus,* Ludwig Wittgenstein wrote: "The sense of the world must lie outside the world. . . . Ethics is transcendental."

Jean Jacques Rousseau, no friend of Christianity, had to concede the same thing: "In order to discover the rules of society best suited to nations, a superior intelligence beholding all the passions of men without experiencing any of them would be needed. This intelligence would have to be wholly unrelated to our nature, while knowing it through and through; its happiness would have to be independent of us, and yet ready to occupy itself with ours; and lastly, it would have, in the march of time, to look forward to a distant glory, and, working in one century, to be able to enjoy in the next. It would take gods to give men laws."

Freud argued that moral laws are important, but he insisted that we get them somewhere else: "The ethical demands on which religion seeks to lay stress need, rather, to be given another basis; for they are indispensable to human society and it is dangerous to link obedience to them with religious faith."

At one point, even Albert Einstein agreed: "A man's ethical behavior should be based effectually on sympathy, education and social ties; no religious basis is necessary. Man would indeed be in a poor way if he had to be restrained by fear of punishment and hope of reward after death."

Yet is it possible to have ethics without belief in God? In *The Story of Civilization,* Will and Ariel Durant wrote: "Moreover, we shall find it no easy task to mold a natural ethic strong enough to maintain moral restraint and social order without the support of supernatural consolations, hopes and fears." Noted Reformed theologian Francis Schaeffer replied: "History, experience, and logic prove that it is not only difficult, as the Durants suggest, but impossible."

Werner Heisenberg, Nobel prize-winning author of the quantum theory, declared: "Religion is . . . the foundation of ethics and ethics is the presupposition of life. For we must make decisions every day and we must know or at least surmise the values which are to govern our action."

Without transcendental religious values, all things *are* permitted. As Dennis Rodman boasted, we can be just as bad as we want to be. Even though at the time Germany boasted the world's strongest and most enlightened academy, under Nietzsche's spell, Adolf Hitler said: "I cannot see why man should not be just as cruel as nature." Indeed, why not?

In an article titled "Crimes Without Conscience," Charles Colson cites news stories of schoolboys surrounding and stabbing to death a ninth grader, of a teenage girl chasing and murdering a woman while onlookers chant "Kill her! Kill her!" and other atrocities. Such incidents show the effects of removing our culture's traditional standards of morality. Colson claims: "A society cannot survive if the demands of human dignity are not written on our hearts from early childhood."

Historian Lord John E. E. D. Acton said much the same thing, speaking of the necessity of taking action to prevent a military state: "No country can be free without religion. It creates and strengthens the sense of duty. If men are not kept straight by duty, they must be by fear. The more they are kept by fear, the less they are free."

Yet, in an attempt to be free, the apostles of atheism advocated the opposite: the overthrow of religion and all other duties (moral constraints). After that, anything goes.

Sir Frederick Catherwood, former vice-president of the European Parliament, writes that each moral order the world has known is different, but the Christian one probably contains the greatest element of personal freedom. Since the individual is directly answerable to God, the Christian order rests to the maximum extent on individual personal responsibility and as little as possible on the sanctions of society and state.

When a society loses its transcendent moral fiber, chaos results. It's every woman for herself, every man doing what is right in his own eyes.

Bertrand Russell lamented: "I cannot . . . refute the arguments for the subjectivity of ethical values, but I find myself incapable of believing that all that is wrong with wanton cruelty is that I don't like it."

Ernest Hemingway explained his moral philosophy this way: "What is moral is what you feel good after and what is immoral is what you feel bad after."

Not bad.

But for Russell, one of the twentieth century's most famous philosophers, to do no better is inexcusable. Yet what are the alternatives?

If Russell admitted God's existence and relevance, he would have had to have lived a much different life. And Russell wasn't prepared to do that. So, cut off from God, he had to invent his own rules, his own morality. And, apart from God, that's a very subjective, fallible—and ultimately impossible—task.

Even Russell had to admit, "Without civic morality communities perish; without personal morality their survival has no value." Morality matters—*but whose morality will it be?*

Several years ago Jamaica faced a grave national crisis. The *Daily Gleaner* reported that from 1961 to 1991 murder increased 950 percent, shootings 4,800 percent, and robbery 2,000 percent. From January to October 1991, 540 murders were committed in this nation of 2.4 million people.

The solution? The governor-general, Sir Howard Cooke, appointed by Queen Elizabeth herself, put it bluntly: "We must evangelize the nation or it will perish."

In Cooke's thinking, the only way to reestablish civic morality in his island nation was to work for the spiritual conversion of its citizens.

He knew, as British history bears out, that contrary to popular thinking national change doesn't start from the top. That's where the extreme right wingers—and extreme left wingers—have it all wrong. Ultimately, it doesn't matter who's president. It matters what—or Who—is present in individuals' hearts.

Despite the loud protests of the apostles of atheism, it's indisputable that God is relevant to the moral order of our lives, families, communities, and nations.

REASON NO. 4: ALL OF THE ABOVE—AND MORE

Atheists certainly have cited other reasons for not believing in God besides the problem of evil and suffering, the rejection of (bad) religion, and the desire for moral independence.

As we've seen, some have used "science" as a club or dismissed the Judeo-Christian Scriptures out of hand. Still others have claimed that God-talk is "cognitively meaningless" or decried the "insufficient evidence" to support theism.

Why such extraordinary efforts to fight against God?

Robert A. Morey, Hans Küng, John P. Koster, and others have documented how each of the apostles of atheism and many of their prominent colleagues over the years have embraced unbelief in God for personal reasons, and only later sought intellectual arguments to support their rejection of and anger toward God.

For instance, Darwin, Huxley, Nietzsche, and Freud, among others, felt a great deal of animosity or hatred toward their fathers, almost all of whom were religious men exhibiting some fault their sons found intolerable. Schopenhauer also may have deeply resented his father, who apparently committed suicide while Arthur was a boy; he certainly felt much bitterness toward his mother. Psychological research by William Glasser and others suggests that severe parent-child alienation often produces negative long-term effects, which was certainly the case for each of these men.

As well, all of these men exhibited an extraordinary amount of pride. One senses this almost immediately in the writings of Descartes, Hegel, Schopenhauer, Feuerbach, Marx, Nietzsche, Freud, Russell, Sartre, and others. After turning from atheism to embrace classic Christianity, C. S. Lewis called pride "the complete anti-God state of mind."

Domenico Grasso noted: "Pride is very seldom self-conscious. The man who is not disposed to follow the call of God will do everything possible to convince himself that such a call does not really exist. Not satisfied with the proof that God gives him, with the signs of credibility with which Jesus and His Apostles have been accredited, man presents God with his conditions: he will believe if God will give him proof in the manner he demands."

Harold Kushner adds: ". . . the original sin, the wrong turn from which so many subsequent mistakes and problems follow, is not disobedience or lust, but the arrogant claim of self-sufficiency, the idea that we don't need help, that we are strong enough to do it entirely on our own." Completely missed by the apostles of atheism is "the very first lesson of religion . . . that we are all spiritually incomplete people and we all have room to grow."

Yet these men weren't theological novices. All were educated and several, including Kant, Hegel, Haeckel, Strauss, Darwin, Feuerbach, Marx, and Nietzsche (and later Joseph Stalin), pursued theological studies. Most of the rest attended universities rich in religious tradition, either Catholic or Protestant. Though raised Protestant, Marx's mother and father were descended from a long line of rabbinical families. Though taught by Catholics, Freud was significantly influenced by his Jewish heritage.

Many of these men also suffered from chronic physical ailments. Schopenhauer was a hypochondriac. Kant had poor health. Marx suffered from a variety of physical complaints. Freud wrestled with cancer of the mouth. Darwin was a semi-invalid by his early thirties. Darwin, Marx, Nietzsche, and Freud all fought violent headaches and severe abdominal complaints. Nietzsche also endured chest injuries, intense eye pain (perhaps related to his syphilitic infection), insomnia, continual vomiting, and (not surprisingly) attacks of depression countered occasionally by euphoric moods and bursts of extraordinary creativity. Hegel, Darwin, Nietzsche, and Freud experienced prolonged severe depression. Feuerbach suffered from severe ill health for many years, but largely after most of his works had been published.

For these and other reasons, most of the apostles of atheism and their colleagues were essentially unhappy men. Such unhappiness, however, was "not a cause but a companion to . . . irresponsible behavior," according to Glasser.

Noted Jewish rabbi Gamaliel warned two millennia ago: "Beware lest you find yourselves fighting against God."

In part, Lewis explains why: "When you are arguing against Him you are arguing against the very power that makes you able to argue at all."

It is time, I contend, for you and me to resolutely and definitively forsake the destructive arguments of the apostles of atheism, and instead actively to promote belief in God through Jesus Christ!

Will you join me toward that end?

JENNY'S STORY

Everyone has his or her reasons for doubting God. Jenny, a skeptical young woman living in London, wrote to tell me:

"I've lived a life many would envy—I worked in TV for many years, mixing with the rich and famous; I have my own flat and a bachelor-girl lifestyle with all the 'freedoms' that implies. But it all meant absolutely nothing. Inside was a hollow and I simply couldn't fill it. I was saturated with thirty years of logic, science and cynicism which had taught me to accept nothing without close examination and proof.

"When your picture began appearing on all the trains and stations in London inviting me to 'bring my doubts' I decided to give it a shot—I had plenty of doubts to bring. On 15 June I went to Queens Park Rangers Stadium. As I sat and listened to you that night you began to get through to me, and I started to get the disturbing feeling that some of what you said might be true. I went home and thought about it for several days and then sat down to write you a letter.

"I began to set out all my arguments as to why I didn't believe in Jesus Christ until, halfway through writing, I realized what I had written wasn't true. I did believe.

"So today I sit writing a very different letter. You introduced me to Jesus and I thank you from the bottom of my heart."

Her letter reminds me of something Philip Yancey said: "One does not expect to find the arguments of God's adversaries . . . bound into the Bible, but nearly all of them make an appearance, if not in Job, then in the Psalms or Prophets. The Bible seems to anticipate our disappointments, as if God grants us in advance the weapons to use against him, as if God himself understands the cost of sustaining faith."

In other words, God isn't surprised when we struggle with unbelief. He isn't shocked when we rage against the evil and suffering all too frequently buffeting those we know and love. He grieves over the sins of the Church even more than we do.

The question isn't, *Are there any valid arguments against God's relevance?* But, *Why am I afraid to consider the possibility of embracing relationship with him?*

EPILOGUE

Big doors really do turn on small hinges.

Have you made your decision yet to open the door of your heart and invite God to come in?

Shortly after the start of World War II, a soldier told his wife "I'll be back soon," then left her and their infant son to head into combat.

Five years went by. The young mother would show her boy a portrait of the soldier and say, "See, that's your daddy. One day he's going to come home." In reality, she didn't know what to expect.

One morning the boy said, "Mommy, wouldn't it be great if Daddy would just step out of the picture frame?"

In a sense that's what God did two thousand years ago. As part of his eternal plan, he stepped out of heaven and became a man so you and I could look at Jesus and say, "That's what God looks like."

THE CRADLE

On the first Christmas almost two thousand years ago, God came to earth to live among us. The human mind is boggled by that. Even more unexpected is the first picture we see. No flaming chariots brought God into the world, and no royal entourage greeted him. God entered the world as a helpless baby with a feeding trough as his bed.

Even though we celebrate this miracle every Christmas, and wonder at the mystery of it, many people don't really think about it or believe it. But if God is God, he can take upon himself a human body.

Jesus Christ was no ordinary man. He was God-become-man. But first he was born of the Virgin Mary by the miracle of the Holy Spirit. Jesus did not evolve from history; he came into history from the outside. His life is the highest and holiest entering the lowest and lowliest. But that was not enough. If Jesus had grown up and lived only a perfect and marvelous life, without another great miracle taking place, his life likely would mean nothing to you and me today.

THE CROSS

Jesus had to go from the cradle to the cross. After Christmas comes Good Friday. The Bible clearly states that the cross was the reason God's Son came to earth. In the mystery and marvel of it, Jesus was willing to go. "And being found in appearance as a man, He humbled Himself and became obedient to death—even death on a cross!" (Philippians 2:8)

What happened on the cross? The Bible teaches that God the Son took upon himself all the sins of the world. Every evil thought you and I have ever pondered; every sin that we have ever committed; every evil, mean, dirty, jealous act that we have practiced, was laid on Jesus Christ.

The Bible calls Jesus "the Lamb of God, who takes away the sin of the world!" (John 1:29). What is it talking about?

In the Old Testament the Lord gave us a vivid picture of what the cross is all about. In those days, if you wanted to get close to God but felt you had a burden of guilt on your conscience, you would take a lamb to the priest at the temple.

The priest would lay your hand on the head of that little lamb, you would confess your sins to God, and ask his forgiveness. The priest would then kill the lamb as an offering to God. Then, the Old Testament teaches, God would forgive you.

That was a picture of what Jesus Christ would do on the cross. He took our sins on his own body. He took my rebellion, my pride, my impurity, my covetousness—every evil thing Luis Palau ever did—and he said, "Luis, I love you! I want you to know I died for you. And if you repent and turn to me, then I will forgive you and cleanse you. Every sin you ever committed will be forgotten forever."

It doesn't matter how rebellious and evil you have been, or how guilty you feel. If you want forgiveness, you must come to the cross. Once you do, you won't have restless nights with a guilty conscience. Instead, you will be able to sing praises to God. You will have peace with God because Jesus is the Lamb of God who takes away the sins of the world.

THE CROWN

The Bible says that Jesus, three days after his death, stepped out of the grave. That's what Easter is all about. Jesus is not in a tomb. Confucius, Buddha, and other religious leaders of yesteryear are dead, buried, and gone. But you can visit Jesus' grave and it's empty.

Jesus is the reigning King of kings and Lord of lords. He's God the Son, with all the power in heaven and on earth. God the Father has given him a "name that is above every name, that at the name of Jesus every knee should bow . . . and every tongue confess that Jesus Christ is Lord" (Philippians 2:9–11).

Have you confessed the Lord Jesus as your Savior? If you haven't, I urge you to stop playing games with your eternal destiny. Commit your life to God's Son. He was born and placed in a humble cradle as a little baby. He died on a Roman cross to take away all the world's guilt and shame. And then, on the third day after he was buried, he stepped out of the grave.

Jesus Christ is alive! He's ruler of heaven and earth. He wants to be your God and King.

YOU CAN STEP OUT

Have you taken the important step of acknowledging Jesus Christ as your God and King? It is the greatest decision of your life. If you haven't made that commitment yet, I encourage you to do so right now.

You may wish to use this prayer: "Heavenly Father, I believe in my heart you raised Jesus from the dead. I believe he was God-become-man. I believe he died for me on the cross. I believe he is crowned at the right hand of God the Father. Thank you for forgiving my sins. I trust Jesus Christ as my Savior. Amen."

As I said at the end of Chapter Seven, the important thing isn't saying the right words, but talking heart-to-heart with the Lord and inviting him in.

If you've done that, congratulations! Please, write and tell me about your decision. If you're still undecided after reading this book, let's dialogue by letter, phone, fax or e-mail.

I look forward to hearing from you.

Luis Palau
P.O. Box 1173, Portland, Oregon 97207, U.S.A.
Telephone: (503) 614-1500
Fax: (503) 614-1599
E-mail: palau@palau.org
Internet: http://www.gospelcom.net/lpea

ACKNOWLEDGMENTS

Scripture reminds us to "give honor to whom honor is due" (Romans 13:7, paraphrase).

My deepest thanks to Russell Chandler, Dr. Keith J. Hardman, Dr. Gordon E. Lewis, Dr. Alister E. McGrath, the Rev. Douglas Salser, the Rev. Robert A. Sirico, and Patricia Donohue-White for the many hours they invested in critiquing the second draft of this book thoroughly and suggesting numerous valuable improvements.

Many others read portions of this book in manuscript form and offered both helpful words of criticism and encouragement, including Julie Cave, the Rev. Dr. Paul Cedar, Dr. Donald E. Chittick, Dick Clark, Jim Falkenberg, the Rev. Ken Gaydos, the Rev. Dr. Eddie Gibbs, Kevin Haislip, the Rev. Jack Hayford, Greg Johnson, Dr. D. James Kennedy, Carol Madison, Greg Matthews, Dr. Daniel Scalberg, and the Rev. Daniel Southern.

I owe a debt of gratitude to my colleagues Ellen Bascuti, Leticia Calçada, Kim Claassen, the Rev. David L. Jones, John Ogle, Mike

Umlandt, the Rev. John Warton, and the Rev. Dr. James M. Williams for all of their assistance.

Special thanks to Alicia Meyer and Katie Rhuman for their research services and to Ruth Steinmetz and Karen Weitzel for their secretarial support.

I wouldn't have attempted a project of this magnitude without the tireless efforts of my coauthor and agent, David Sanford. Together, it's our prayer that each reader discover personally that God is immensely relevant to every area of life, now and for eternity.

LIMITATIONS OF THIS BOOK

I agree with Ravi Zacharias that "many a book will never be written because the author wanted it to be the last word on the subject." I know so much more could have been said in this particular book:

- *about various wisdom traditions outside Christianity, particularly Islam and Judaism.* I've offered only the briefest sketches in Chapter 1, knowing that readers can avail themselves of any of a number of excellent volumes on comparative religion.
- *about the pivotal periods of philosophical development.* It's beyond the scope of this work to describe the role played by Plato as a transitional figure from the ancient world to early Christian thought, or to discuss the transition from medieval to modern thought, let alone to detail what modern thought came to encompass in Europe, say, during the seventeenth century.
- *about the serious theological differences regarding the Gospel message, the sacraments, the creeds, and other issues that still divide the Church five hundred years after the Reformation.* Thankfully, critically nec-

essary dialogue has begun to take place among Christians of various denominations. I certainly am no advocate of individualistic Christianity. I must admit, however, that I find denominational labels far less helpful than recommending particular local churches (as noted at the end of Chapter 7).

- *about the broader philosophical, political, and psychoanalytic thinking of Feuerbach, Marx, Nietzsche, Freud, and others* described in Part III. I've deliberately focused on what each of these men said specifically about God and religion.
- *about other influential atheists,* particularly from the eighteenth and twentieth centuries.
- *about science, truth, revelation,* and many other subjects, including the Gospel itself.

Please see the selected bibliography that follows.

SELECTED BIBLIOGRAPHY

Adler, Mortimer J. *How to Think About God.* New York: Macmillan, 1980.

Angeles, Peter, ed. *Critiques of God.* Buffalo, N.Y.: Prometheus Books, 1976.

Berman, Philip. "Search for Meaning." *Parade,* April 7, 1996, 21–22.

Bready, J. Wesley. *England: Before and After Wesley.* London: Hodder & Stoughton, n.d.

Breese, Dave. *Seven Men Who Rule the World from the Grave.* Chicago: Moody Press, 1990.

Buckley, Michael J. *At the Origins of Modern Atheism.* New Haven: Yale University Press, 1987.

Catherwood, Sir Frederick. *A Better Way.* Leicester, England: Inter-Varsity Press, 1975.

Chandler, Russell. *Racing Toward 2001.* Grand Rapids, Mich.: Zondervan, 1992.

Davies, Rupert E., ed. *We Believe in God.* London: George Allen & Unwin, 1968.

———. "The Harmony of the Spheres." *Time,* February 5, 1996, 58.

Durant, Will and Ariel, *The Lessons of History.* New York: Simon and Schuster, 1968.

———. *The Story of Civilization*, 11 vols. New York: Simon and Schuster, 1975.

Edwards, Paul, ed. *The Encyclopedia of Philosophy.* 8 vols. New York: Macmillan and Free Press, 1967.

Fabro, Cornelio. *God in Exile.* Westminster, Md.: Newman Press, 1964.

Gerstner, John H. *Reasons for Faith.* Grand Rapids, Mich.: Baker Book House, 1967. (Originally published by Harper & Row.)

Graham, Billy. *Facing Death—And the Life After.* Waco, Tex.: Word Books, 1987.

———. *Peace with God*, revised and expanded. Waco, Texas: Word Books, 1984 (originally published in 1953).

Grasso, Domenico. *Proclaiming God's Message.* Notre Dame, Ind.: University of Notre Dame Press, 1965.

Green, Michael. *Evangelism in the Early Church.* Grand Rapids, Mich.: Eerdmans, 1970.

Halverson, Richard C. *The Timelessness of Jesus Christ.* Ventura, Calif.: Regal Books, 1982.

Hardman, Keith J. *Seasons of Refreshing.* Grand Rapids, Mich.: Baker Book House, 1995.

Hayward, Alan. *God Is.* Nashville: Nelson, 1978.

Hewitt, Hugh (host). *Searching for God in America.* On videocassette, 3 vols. Alexandria, Va.: PBS Home Video, 1996.

Hirsch, E. D., Jr., et al. *The Dictionary of Cultural Literacy.* Boston: Houghton Mifflin, 1988.

Holton, Susan, and David L. Jones. *Spirit Aflame.* Grand Rapids, Mich.: Baker Book House, 1985.

Houghton, John. *Does God Play Dice?* Grand Rapids, Mich.: Zondervan, 1989.

Hume, David. *The Natural History of Religion.* London: Oxford University Press, 1976.

Johnson, B. C. *The Atheist Debater's Handbook.* Buffalo, N.Y.: Prometheus Books, 1983.

Johnstone, Patrick. *Operation World.* 5th ed. Grand Rapids, Mich.: Zondervan, 1993.

Kennedy, D. James, and Jerry Newcombe. *What If Jesus Had Never Been Born?* Nashville: Nelson, 1994.

Kimball, Roger. "A Painful Sting Within the Academic Hive." *Wall Street Journal,* May 29, 1996.

Koivisto, Rex A. *One Lord, One Faith.* Wheaton, Ill.: Victor Books, 1993.

Koster, John P. *The Atheist Syndrome.* Brentwood, Tenn.: Wolgemuth & Hyatt, 1989.

Kreeft, Peter. *Between Heaven and Hell.* Downers Grove, Ill.: InterVarsity Press, 1982.

Küng, Hans. *Does God Exist?* New York: Crossroad Publishing Company, 1991. (Formerly published in America by Doubleday, 1980. Originally published in German.)

Kushner, Harold. *Who Needs God.* New York: Simon & Schuster, 1989.

LaHaye, Tim. *Jesus, Who Is He?* Sisters, Oreg.: Questar, 1997.

Latourette, Kenneth Scott. *A History of the Expansion of Christianity.* 7 vols. Grand Rapids, Mich.: Zondervan, 1970. (First published by Harper & Row, 1937–45.)

Lewis, C. S. *Mere Christianity.* New York: Macmillian, 1960.

Little, Paul. *Know What You Believe.* Wheaton, Ill.: Victor Books, 1970.

———. *Know Why You Believe.* Wheaton, Ill.: Victor Books, 1967.

Lowenstein, Roger. *Buffett: The Making of an American Capitalist.* New York: Random House, 1995.

McDowell, Josh. *Evidence That Demands a Verdict.* San Bernardino, Calif.: Campus Crusade for Christ International, 1972.

Magida, Arthur J. *How to Be a Perfect Stranger.* Woodstock, Vt.: Jewish Lights, 1996.

Martin, Michael. *Atheism: A Philosophical Justification.* Philadelphia: Temple University Press, 1990.

Miethe, Terry, and Antony Flew. *Does God Exist?* New York: HarperCollins, 1991.

Mitchell, Curtis. *God in the Garden.* Garden City, N.Y.: Doubleday, 1957.

Montgomery, John W. *Human Rights and Human Dignity.* Grand Rapids, Mich.: Zondervan, 1986.

Moreland, J. P., and Kai Nielsen. *Does God Exist?* Nashville: Nelson, 1990.

Morey, Robert A. *The New Atheism and the Erosion of Freedom.* Minneapolis, Minn.: Bethany House, 1986.

Morris, Thomas V., ed. *God and the Philosophers.* New York: Oxford University Press, 1994.

Moyers, Bill (host). *The Wisdom of Faith with Huston Smith.* On videocassette, 5 vols. Princeton, N.J.: Films for the Humanities, 1996.

Murray, Jon Garth. *Essays on American Atheism.* Austin, Tex.: American Atheist Press, 1986.

Nielsen, Kai. *Philosophy and Atheism: In Defense of Atheism.* Buffalo, N.Y.: Prometheus Books, 1985.

Oden, Thomas C. "Why We Believe in Heresy," *Christianity Today,* March 4, 1996, 12–13.

Orwell, George. *1984* (with preface by Walter Cronkite). New York: New American Library, 1983.

Packer, J. I., and Thomas Howard. *Christianity: The True Humanism.* Waco, Tex.: Word Inc., 1985.

Palau, Luis, with David Sanford. *Calling America and the Nations to Christ.* Nashville: Nelson, 1994.

———. *What Is a Real Christian?* Portland, Oreg.: Multnomah Press, 1985. (Published in thirty-two languages worldwide.)

Peck, M. Scott. *People of the Lie.* New York: Simon & Schuster, 1983.

Pursuit. Vol. IV, no. 4. 901 East 78th St., Minneapolis, Minn. 55420-1360; toll-free 1-800-995-5360.

Raeburn, Paul. "Junk Science and Mass Hysteria." *Business Week,* April 8, 1996, 35.

Richardson, Don. *Eternity in Their Hearts.* Ventura, Calif.: Regal Books, 1981.

Robinson, Richard. *An Atheist's Values.* London: Oxford University Press, 1964.

Ross, Hugh. *The Creator and the Cosmos.* Colorado Springs, Colo.: NavPress, 1993.

Schaeffer, Francis A. *How Should We Then Live?* Old Tappan, N.J.: Revell, 1976.

———. *The God Who Is There.* Downers Grove, Ill.: InterVarsity Press, 1968.

Schaff, Philip. *History of the Christian Church.* 8 vols. Grand Rapids, Mich.: Eerdmans, n.d. (First published in 1866.)

Scharpff, Paulus. *History of Evangelism.* Grand Rapids, Mich.: Eerdmans, 1966. (Originally published in German.)

Schwarz, Hans. *The Search for God.* Minneapolis, Minn.: Augsburg, 1975.

Sproul, R. C. *Classical Apologetics.* Grand Rapids, Mich.: Zondervan, 1984.

———. *Lifeviews.* Old Tappan, N.J.: Revell, 1986.

———. *If There Is a God, Why Are There Atheists?* Minneapolis, Minn.: Bethany Fellowship, 1978. (Originally published under the title *The Psychology of Atheism.*)

Stein, Gordon, ed. *An Anthology of Atheism and Rationalism.* Buffalo, N.Y.: Prometheus Books, 1980.

———, ed. *The Encyclopedia of Unbelief.* 2 vols. Buffalo, N.Y.: Prometheus Books, 1985.

Stott, John R. W. *Basic Christianity.* Downers Grove, Ill.: InterVarsity Press, 1964.

———. *The Cross of Christ.* Leicester, England: Inter-Varsity Press, 1986.

Strobel, Lee. *Inside the Mind of Unchurched Harry and Mary.* Grand Rapids, Mich.: Zondervan, 1993.

Triton, A. N. *Whose World.* London: Inter-Varsity Press, 1970.

Tucker, Ruth A. *From Jerusalem to Irian Jaya: A Biographical History of Christian Missions.* Grand Rapids, Mich.: Zondervan, 1983.

Wells, David F. *God in the Wasteland.* Grand Rapids, Mich.: Eerdmans, 1994.

White, David Manning. *The Search for God.* New York: Macmillan, 1983.

Woodbridge, John, ed. *More Than Conquerors: Portraits of Believers from All Walks of Life.* Chicago: Moody Press, 1992.

Zacharias, Ravi. *Can Man Live Without God?* Dallas: Word Publishing, 1994.

———. *A Shattered Visage: The Real Face of Atheism.* Grand Rapids, Mich.: Baker Book House, 1990.